Jost Nickel's
GROOVE BOOK

Groove Design
Orchestration
Split & Switch Grooves
Linear Grooves
Ghost Notes
Displacements
Bass Drum:
Technics & Control
Go-Go Grooves
Timing
and much more

CD INSIDE

MORE THAN 200 MP3 GROOVES AND EXERCISES

Alfred Music
LEARN • TEACH • PLAY

© 2015 by **Alfred** Music Publishing GmbH
info@alfredverlag.de
alfredverlag.de | alfredmusic.de
alfred.com | alfredUK.com
All Rights Reserved
Printed in Germany

Cover design: Thomas Petzold
Engraving: Jost Nickel
Editor: Thomas Petzold
Head of production: Thomas Petzold
Item #: 20249US (book & CD)
ISBN-10: 3-943638-90-1
ISBN-13: 978-3-943638-90-5

CD Recording: Jost Nickel
Mix: Kaspar Wiens a.k.a. Tropf
Cover photo and photos on pages 3, 6, 39, 88, and 124 by © Inga Seevers
Pages 22, 32, 44, 75 © Marco Hammer
Page 60 © Nils Müller

Thanks

My particular thanks go to:

Harald Wester for his great advice, precise work, and endurance.

Sonor Drums: Thomas Barth, Karl-Heinz Menzel, and to my "on-the-road team":
Mattias Mücke and Wolfgang Ulbrich

Meinl Cymbals & Percussion: Norbert Saemann, Chris Brewer, Stephan Hänisch, and Marcus Lipperer

Vic Firth Sticks: Joe Testa and Frank Rohe (M&T)

Remo Drumheads: Chris Hart, Gary Mann, and Nico Nevermann (Gewa)

Ahead Armor Cases: Curt Doernberg (Musik Wein)

Beyerdynamic Microphones: Bernd Neubauer

I dedicate this book to my wife, **Mareike**, and my daughter, **Alma**.

www.jostnickel.com

Jost Nickel's GROOVE BOOK
Preface

I am delighted that you are holding my book in your hands.

You're most welcome!

The title *Groove Book* tells its own tale: This book is exclusively about groove.

I decided upon *Groove* as the topic for my first book because I have fun playing and listening to grooves on the one hand, and then on the other hand, I find drummers most fascinating when they get into a great groove.

All grooves in this book will sound great and be fun to play.

Additionally, it was important to me to show you a range of possibilties for creating your own great-sounding grooves, and how to play these grooves in different ways to expand your own pattern repertoire.

I tried to keep the text passages to a minimum because we all like to start playing the notes rather than reading the words—right?

But that said, I ask you to read the explanations carefully, especially those that focus on the development of your own grooves; I know they will be helpful.

How to Work with This Book:

Please take your time after studying each chapter to reflect on its contents:

• What are the key points to highlight?
• What did you most enjoy?
• Can you transfer these concepts to another context?

Please free yourself from the music notation as soon as possible. Frequently you are able to play things by heart very quickly, without reference to the music text. The moment you can play by heart you are free to listen to your own playing more consciously, and you will be able to pay more attention to technical and musical details.

I'm sure you will find certain grooves that you like best in each chapter. Mark your favorite grooves and add those to your own groove repertoire.

Have fun working with my book!

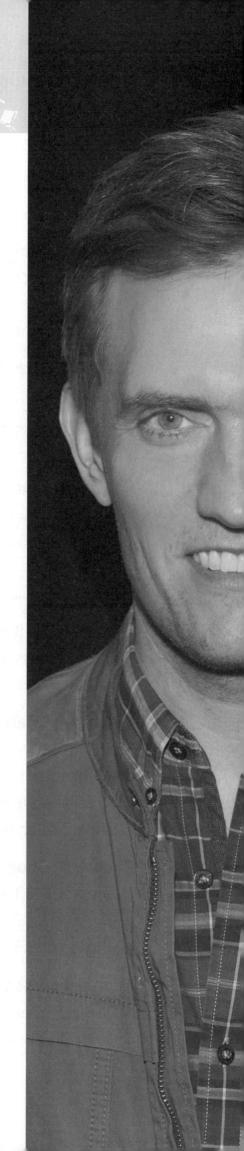

Contents

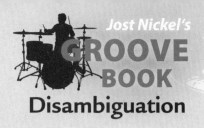

What Is "Groove" Actually About?

Especially in the context of drumming, the term "groove" has two basic, different meanings. On one hand, "groove" is used in order to describe *what* is played. If you hear an interesting pattern you can also say: "This is a good groove."

But when it is also about *how* to play, the term "groove" can be used, too. In case you say that a drummer has a good groove, it means that his playing feels very good. This feeling starts with the musician himself, is transmitted to the accompanying musicians, and then goes to the audience.

Independent of which instrument is played, those musicians whose playing creates the best feeling, "the best groove," are always most favored.

In a band, all musicians are responsible for the groove, but we drummers bear the biggest responsibility for the groove.

When you start to work with the different grooves in this book, the first question will always be what do I play? You will practice new beat sequences, new stickings, and unfamiliar ways to orchestrate. But please don't forget how to play each new groove. Play each pattern until there are no more problems and it feels dead easy. To make a long story short, practice each pattern until it feels right and it is really grooving. Be sure that each groove activity will result in a better groove!

The Drumset Notation in This Book

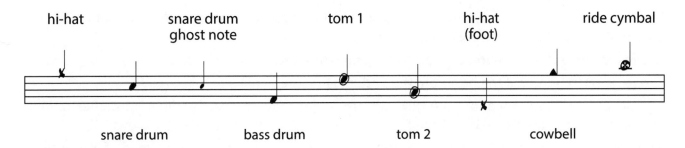

How to Count Rhythms in This Book

Whole Note

Half Notes

Quarter Notes (4ths)

Eighth Notes (8ths)

Sixteenth Notes (16ths)

1 e + a 2 e + a 3 e + a 4 e + a

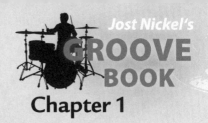

Chapter 1

Orchestration Concepts – The Split and the Switch

In the beginning of this book, I introduce you to two basic concepts of orchestration that I will come back to in some of the following chapters.

Orchestration is the allocation of beats to single instruments of the drumset.

The target is to bring out the best from the patterns that are familiar to you already.

Instead of learning more and more new patterns, I vary my grooves by different orchestrations, accentuation, and the like to be able to find more alternatives of rhythmic expressions.

In order to learn both orchestration concepts, start with a sticking you are already familiar with. Let's start with one of the most popular stickings: **the paradiddle**.

Paradiddle – Groove A

Ghost note[1]
R = right hand
L = left hand

For a good sound, it's important that you take care of the hi-hat accents. I play the first stroke of the double strokes on the hi-hat in a softer volume than the second stroke. The first exercise shows these differentiated accents, but in the following exercises I won't show the accents anymore to keep the reading text clear.

If I play these grooves on the ride cymbal, I play the accents on the bell and the unaccented strokes about one inch to the left. I realize this motion from the wrist. My arm doesn't really shift.

Paradiddle – Groove B

Track 1

---

[1] *Ghost notes are an excellent way to expand the dynamic range of your playing. Ghost notes (smaller note heads) are played at a very soft volume. To create this sound, strike the snare from a lower stick height. For more detailed information, please refer to the section on ghost notes starting on page 49.*

The Split

The first orchestration variant is **The Split**:

The strokes in the right hand are divided between the hi-hat and the ride cymbal.

The right hand always plays alternately on the hi-hat and ride throughout. Place your right hand between the hi-hat and ride cymbal, so that you hardly have to move your arm and the movement originates in your wrist.

The Split 1
Track 2

R L R R L R L L R L R R L R L L

In the next example, the right hand continues to play the ride cymbal and hi-hat alternately. Here, the first beat is now on the ride cymbal and the second on the hi-hat, etc.

The Split 2
Track 3

R L R R L R L L R L R R L R L L

In the next two examples, the pattern in the right hand is divided between the hi-hat and floor tom, beginning with the hi-hat:

The Split 3
Track 4

R L R R L R L L R L R R L R L L

Here it is also worthwhile to begin with the floor tom instead of the hi-hat:

The Split 4
Track 5

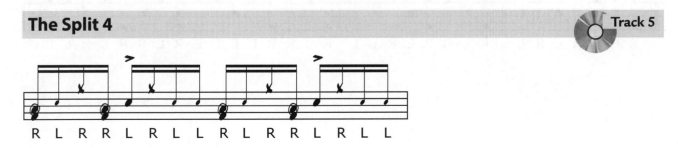

R L R R L R L L R L R R L R L L

The Switch

The second orchestration variant is **The Switch**, which is performed as follows:

The right and left hands change instruments.

The right hand now plays the snare and the left hand the hi-hat. This is a different orchestration, in which the sticking and bass drum pattern are retained. The right hand therefore begins on the snare.

The Switch 1

Before switching our hands, the snare accents were on **2** and **4**. This will no longer work, as the snare is now not played on those beats. For this reason, we have to search for new accents.

The Switch 2   Track 6

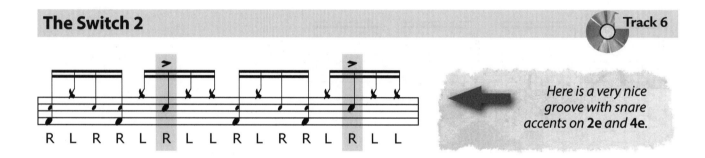

*Here is a very nice groove with snare accents on **2e** and **4e**.*

Now we progress to combinations:

In measure 1, the right hand plays the hi-hat. In measure 2, we then perform the Switch.

The Switch 3   Track 7

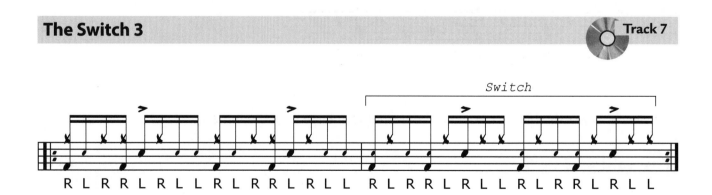

In the following example, the right hand plays the snare in measure 1 and then changes in measure 2 to the hi-hat.

The Switch 4

Track 8

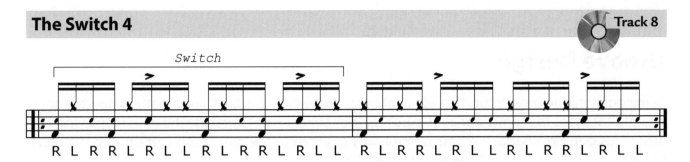

R L R R L R L L R L R R L R L L   R L R R L R L L R L R R L R L L

Now we come to the **one-bar versions** of the Switch.

In the first half of the measure, the right hand plays the hi-hat and changes in the middle of the measure to the snare.

The Switch 5

Track 9

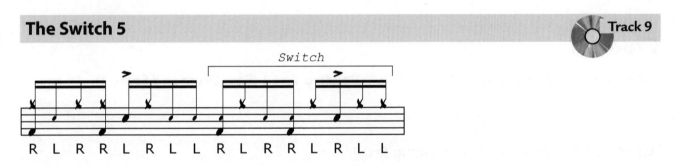

R L R R L R L L R L R R L R L L

The next example, **The Switch 6**, is my favorite groove in this chapter. The right hand begins on the snare and changes on **3** to the hi-hat.

The Switch 6

Track 10
Track 11

R L R R L R L L R L R R L R L L

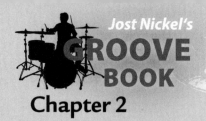
Groove Design

In my opinion, the most important elements of a groove are the bass drum pattern and the snare accents: these are the cornerstones of a groove. They almost always provide the basis for playing with other musicians in a band. The bass is frequently oriented to the bass drum pattern, and the guitar possibly also joins in with the snare accents on **2** and **4**.

The hi-hat pattern and ghost notes characterize the underlying feeling of a groove. Is the feeling based, for example, on quarter notes, eighth notes, or sixteenth notes?

On top of a solid foundation consisting of bass drum and snare, you can play wonderful ghost notes and interesting hi-hat patterns.

This chapter focuses on different approaches in which the constant elements of bass drum and snare can be complemented with hi-hat patterns and ghost notes.

Groove 1

The basis for our first groove is Measure 1 from **Reading Text 1 (Bass Drum and Snare 1)**.

Groove 1A = Measure 1 from Reading Text 1

1 e + a 2 e + a 3 e + a 4 e + a

Groove 1B | plus eighth notes on the hi-hat

Groove 1C | plus ghost notes

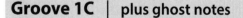

Track 12

How this ghost note pattern is formed is explained in detail in **Chapter 5 Ghost Notes** *beginning on page 52.*

You should focus on the following when playing **grooves with ghost notes**:

1. Dynamics: Ghost notes are played very softly—accents, in contrast, very loudly.

Dynamics are achieved by creating the correct distance between the stick and the drumhead. When playing ghost notes, the stick should be about one-half to one inch above the drumhead. Accents are played at a substantially greater distance to the drumskin, mostly with rimshots.

2. Ghost Note Technique: Play the ghost notes from your wrist, not with your fingers.

The stick control with your fingers requires a greater distance to the drumhead than the ghost note distance (one-half to one inch). Attempts to play ghost notes with your fingers mostly result in inaccurately placed ghost notes.

In the following new version of our groove, the hi-hat plays an intermittent sixteenth-note pattern. The left hand fills up the gaps in the hi-hat with snare accents and ghost notes. Bass drum and snare accents remain unchanged.

Groove 1D

R L R R L R L R R L R R L R R L

 *How I create ghost note and hi-hat patterns is explained in **Chapter 3 Do It Yourself** on page 33.*

Do not forget about the accents on the hi-hat! When playing double strokes on the hi-hat or ride cymbal, I play the first stroke **softer** than the second one.

Groove 1E | Groove with Accents on the Hi-Hat   Track 13

R L R R L R L R R L R R L R R L

The Split

Now we focus on the orchestration possibilities that I explained in *chapter 1* **Paradiddle Groove** (*see page 8*). First, **the Split**:

We divide the hi-hat pattern between the hi-hat and ride cymbal. The pattern itself and the sticking remain unchanged, but the right hand alternately plays the hi-hat and ride cymbal.

The right hand begins on the hi-hat, then plays the ride cymbal, and then goes back to the hi-hat, etc.

Groove 1 – Split 1

R L R R L R L R R L R R L R R L

Groove 1 – Split 2 | The Right Hand Begins on the Ride Cymbal:

R L R R L R L R R L R R L R R L

In the next example, the same principle is orchestrated differently. This time, the right hand is divided between the hi-hat and floor tom.

Groove 1 – Split 3 | The Right Hand Begins on the Hi-Hat:

R L R R L R L R R L R R L R R L

Groove 1 – Split 4 | The Right Hand Begins on the Floor Tom:

R L R R L R L R R L R R L R R L

Up until now, we have always utilized the Split over an entire measure. In the next pair of two-bar versions of this groove, the concept is employed in a slightly more flexible fashion.

The Split only appears briefly and does not begin on the first beat, as before.

Split grooves with hi-hat and ride cymbal:

Groove 1 – Split 5 — Track 18

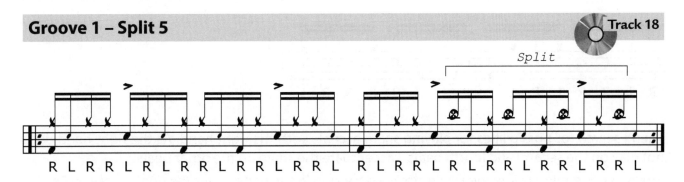

Groove 1 – Split 6 — Track 19

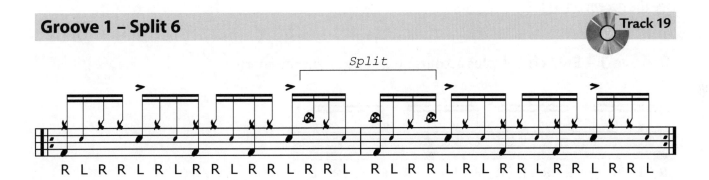

Split grooves with hi-hat and floor tom:

Groove 1 – Split 7 — Track 20

Groove 1 – Split 8 — Track 21

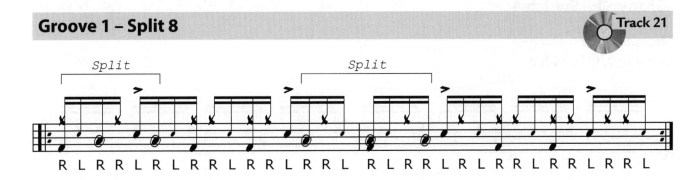

The Switch

The hands swap instruments: the right hand plays the snare and the left hand the hi-hat.

Groove 1 – Switch 1

R L R R L R L R R L R R L R R L

Then I search for possibilities for playing snare accents with the right hand. As the right hand does not play on the second and fourth beats, I accentuate the snare on the other beats.

Wherever possible, I utilize the single strokes occurring in the pattern (*see the single stroke on* **2e**).

Generally, it is naturally also good to play accents on the first or second stroke of a double stroke (*see the accent on* **4+**).

Groove 1 – Switch 2 | plus accents on 2e and 4+ on the snare

Track 22

R L R R L R L R R L R R L R R L

In order to be able to employ the Switch flexibly, we combine the "normal" way of playing ("normal" = right hand plays hi-hat) with the Switch in two-bar grooves.

Groove 1 – Switch 3

Track 23

Measure 1: RH = hi-hat
Measure 2: RH = snare

R L R R L R L R R L R R L R R L   R L R R L R L R R L R R L R R L

Groove 1 – Switch 4

Track 24

Measure 1: RH = snare
Measure 2: RH = hi-hat

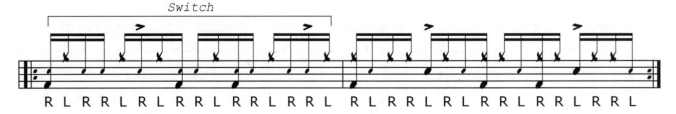

R L R R L R L R R L R R L R R L   R L R R L R L R R L R R L R R L

One-bar combinations also sound good with the Switch. Basically, I swap my hands on **3**. If a double stroke is planned for the third beat, this double stroke remains on one instrument, i.e. either on the snare or the hi-hat.

In the next groove, the right hand therefore changes as early as on **2a** from the hi-hat to the snare.

Groove 1 – Switch 5

R L R R L R L R R L R R L R R L

Groove 1 – Switch 6 | LH plays hi-hat and changes on 3e to the snare:

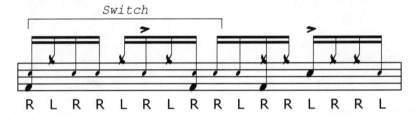

R L R R L R L R R L R R L R R L

Here are a pair of two-bar Switch grooves (these are combinations from the examples **Groove 1 – Switch 5** and **Groove 1 – Switch 6**):

Groove 1 – Switch 7

Track 27

R L R R L R L R R L R R L R R L   R L R R L R L R R L R R L R R L

Groove 1 – Switch 8

Track 28
Track 29

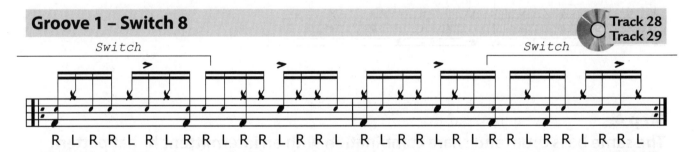

R L R R L R L R R L R R L R R L   R L R R L R L R R L R R L R R L

Six Steps to Bass Drum and Snare Combinations

We have augmented a constant bass drum and snare combination with hi-hat patterns and ghost notes in different ways.

Step 1: Select a bass drum and snare combination
Step 2: plus hi-hat pattern
Step 3: plus ghost notes
Step 4: Intermittent hi-hat pattern plus ghost notes
Step 5: The Split
Step 6: The Switch

We will now utilize these **six steps** on three additional bass drum and snare combinations.

Groove 2

Step 1: Select a Bass Drum and Snare Combination

Groove 2A = Measure 2 from Reading Text 1

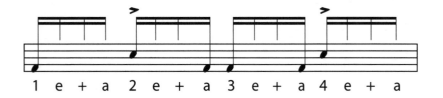

1 e + a 2 e + a 3 e + a 4 e + a

Step 2: Plus Hi-Hat Pattern

Groove 2B | plus eighth notes on the hi-hat

Step 3: Plus Ghost Notes

Groove 2C  Track 30

Step 4:
The same bass drum and snare combination with an intermittent hi-hat pattern plus ghost notes.

Groove 2D Track 31

R R L R L R L R R L L R L R R L

Step 5: The Split

Video-Trailer
This QR Code will lead you to a video about The Split.

Groove 2 – Split 1 | The right hand alternates between hi-hat and ride cymbal.

R R L R L R L R R L L R L R R L

Groove 2 – Split 2 | The right hand alternates between ride cymbal and hi-hat.

R R L R L R L R R L L R L R R L

Groove 2 – Split 3 | The right hand alternates between hi-hat and floor tom.

R R L R L R L R R L L R L R R L

Groove 2 – Split 4 | The right hand alternates between floor tom and hi-hat.

R R L R L R L R R L L R L R R L

The following example **Groove 2 – Split 5** displays a **two-bar** Split groove. The right hand alternates back and forth between the ride cymbal and hi-hat. With this groove, you will automatically land on the ride cymbal on the first beat of the second measure.

Groove 2 – Split 5 | The right hand alternates between hi-hat and ride cymbal. Track 36

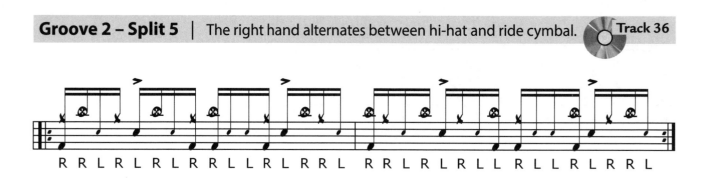

Groove 2 – Split 6 | The right hand alternates between hi-hat and floor tom. Track 37

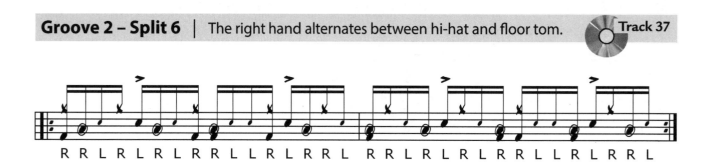

The examples **Groove 2 – Split 7** and **Groove 2 – Split 8** display **two-bar** Split grooves, in which the Split only appears briefly.

Split groove with hi-hat and ride cymbal:

Groove 2 – Split 7 Track 38

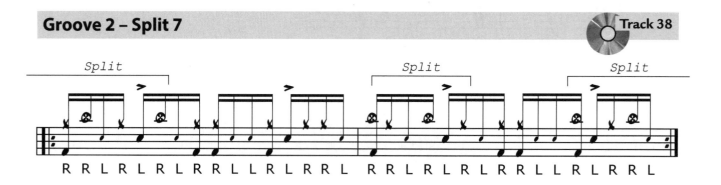

Split groove with hi-hat and floor tom:

Groove 2 – Split 8 Track 39

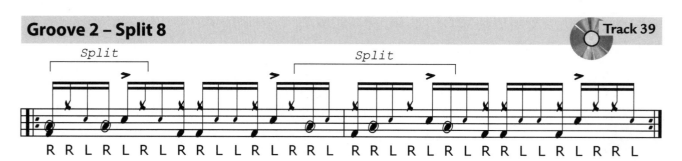

Step 6: The Switch

The hands change instruments: in the Switch, the right hand plays the snare and the left hand the hi-hat. The sticking remains unchanged.

Video-Trailer
This QR Code will lead you to a video about The Switch.

Groove 2 – Switch 1 | First you play the pattern without accents on the snare.

R R L R L R L R R L L R L R R L

Groove 2 – Switch 2 | Now you add the snare accents (here on **1a** and **4+**).

Track 40

R R L R L R L R R L L R L R R L

Once you have become accustomed to the Switch groove with accents, you should practice playing this groove alternately in customary fashion (right hand plays hi-hat) and as a Switch groove.

Groove 2 – Switch 3   Track 41

Measure 1: RH = hi-hat
Measure 2: RH = snare

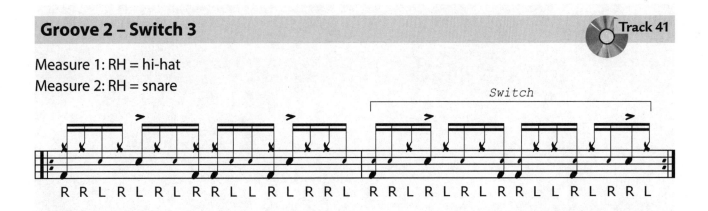

R R L R L R L R R L L R L R R L   R R L R L R L R R L L R L R R L

Groove 2 – Switch 4   Track 42

Measure 1: RH = snare
Measure 2: RH = hi-hat

R R L R L R L R R L L R L R R L   R R L R L R L R R L L R L R R L

To round off, we will play **one-bar Switch grooves**. In the first half of the measure, the right hand plays the hi-hat and the left hand the snare. You then swap your hands from **3e** onwards. The right hand plays the snare and the left hand the hi-hat.

It would be possible to change the orchestration exactly on the third beat, but then the double stroke on **2a** and **3** in the right hand would have to be divided between the hi-hat and the snare, which would not be good for the playability of this groove.

If a double stroke comes on the third beat—as in this groove—the double stroke remains on one instrument.

Groove 2 – Switch 5

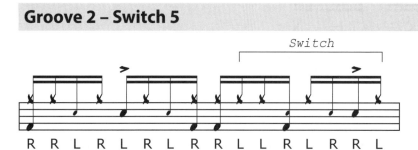

In a second one-bar Switch groove, the right hand plays on the snare in the first half of the measure. As in the example **Groove 2 – Switch 6**, the hands change instruments from **3e** onwards.

Groove 2 – Switch 6

Track 44
Track 45

Groove 3

Step 1: Select a Bass Drum and Snare Combination

For the grooves below, we utilize **Reading Text 2**.

Reading Text 2 provides grooves in which the snare accents occur on beats other than **2** and **4**, as was previously the case.

Groove 3A = Measure 1 from **Reading Text 2** with snare accents on **1a** and **4**

1   e   +   a   2   e   +   a   3   e   +   a   4   e   +   a

Step 2: Plus Hi-Hat Pattern

Groove 3B │ plus eighth notes on the hi-hat

Step 3: Plus Ghost Notes

Groove 3C

Step 4:

The same bass drum and snare combination with an intermittent hi-hat pattern plus ghost notes.

Groove 3D

R   L   R   L   R   R   L   R   R   L   R   R   L   R   R   L

Step 5: The Split

Groove 3 – Split 1 | The right hand alternates between hi-hat and ride cymbal. Track 48

R L R L R R L R R L R R L R R L

Groove 3 – Split 2 | The right hand alternates between ride cymbal and hi-hat. Track 49

R L R L R R L R R L R R L R R L

Groove 3 – Split 3 | The right hand alternates between hi-hat and floor tom.  Track 50

R L R L R R L R R L R R L R R L

Groove 3 – Split 4 | The right hand alternates between floor tom and hi-hat.  Track 51

R L R L R R L R R L R R L R R L

Up until now, we have always utilized the Split over the whole measure. In the next pair of two-bar versions of these grooves, the idea is employed in a more flexible manner. The Split only appears briefly and, unlike before, does not always begin on **1**.

Split grooves with hi-hat and ride cymbal:

Groove 3 – Split 5
Track 52

Groove 3 – Split 6
Track 53

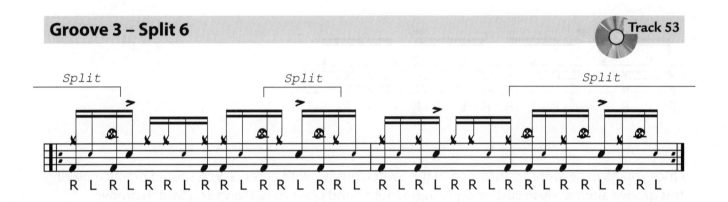

Split grooves with hi-hat and floor tom:

Groove 3 – Split 7
Track 54

Groove 3 – Split 8
Track 55

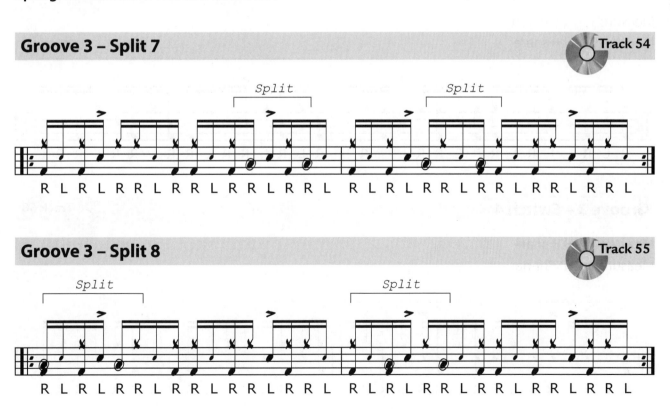

Step 6: The Switch

The hands change instruments: the right hand plays snare on the Switch and the left hand the hi-hat. The sticking remains unchanged.

Groove 3 – Switch 1 | First you play the pattern without accents on the snare.

R L R L R R L R R L R R L R R L

Groove 3 – Switch 2 | Now you add snare accents (here, on **2** and **3a**).

Track 56

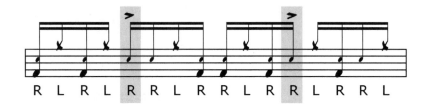

R L R L R R L R R L R R L R R L

Once you have become accustomed to the Switch groove with accents, you should practice playing this groove alternately in customary fashion (right hand plays hi-hat) and as a Switch groove.

Groove 3 – Switch 3

Track 57

Measure 1: RH = hi-hat
Measure 2: RH = snare

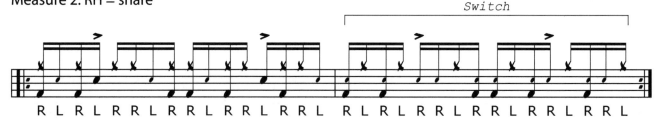

R L R L R R L R R L R R L R R L   R L R L R R L R R L R R L R R L

Groove 3 – Switch 4

Track 58

Measure 1: RH = snare
Measure 2: RH = hi-hat

R L R L R R L R R L R R L R R L   R L R L R R L R R L R R L R R L

We finish with one-bar Switch grooves. In the first half of the measure, the right hand plays the hi-hat and the left hand the snare. From **2a**, you swap hands: the right hand plays the snare and the left hand the hi-hat.

You could alter the orchestration exactly on the third beat, but you would then have to divide the double stroke on **2a** and **3** in the right hand between hi-hat and snare; this is not good for playability.

If, as in this groove, a double stroke occurs on the third beat, this double stroke is played on one instrument.

Groove 3 – Switch 5   Track 59

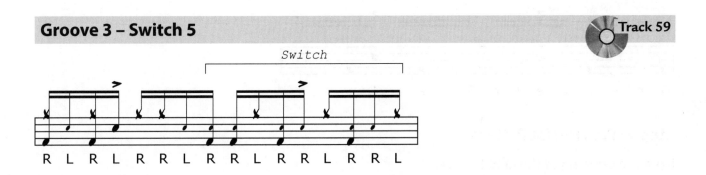

In the example **Groove 3 – Switch 6**, the right hand plays the snare in the first half of the measure. The hands are swapped from **3e** to the end of the measure.

Groove 3 – Switch 6   Track 60
                                                                                  Track 61

Groove 4

Step 1: Select a Bass Drum and Snare Combination

We will take **Reading Text 2** as the basis for Groove 4. This produces grooves in which the snare accents are on beats other than **2** and **4**.

Groove 4A = Measure 2 from Reading Text 2 with snare accents on 2e and 4

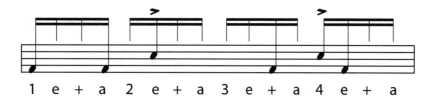

1   e   +   a   2   e   +   a   3   e   +   a   4   e   +   a

Step 2: Plus Hi-Hat Pattern

Note the opening of the hi-hat on **4+**.

Groove 4B | plus eighth notes on the hi-hat

○ = open hi-hat

Step 3: Plus Ghost Notes

Groove 4C   Track 62

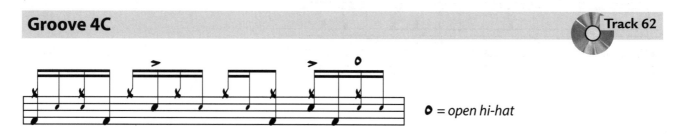

○ = open hi-hat

Step 4:
The same bass drum and snare combination with an intermittent hi-hat pattern plus ghost notes.

Groove 4D   Track 63

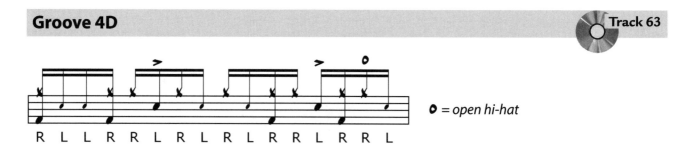

○ = open hi-hat

R   L   L   R   R   L   R   L   R   L   R   R   L   R   R   L

Step 5: The Split

Groove 4 – Split 1 | The right hand alternates between hi-hat and ride cymbal.    **Track 64**

O = *open hi-hat*

R L L R R L R L R L R R L R R L

Groove 4 – Split 2 | The right hand alternates between ride cymbal and hi-hat.    **Track 65**

R L L R R L R L R L R R L R R L

Groove 4 – Split 3 | The right hand alternates between hi-hat and floor tom.    **Track 66**

O = *open hi-hat*

R L L R R L R L R L R R L R R L

Groove 4 – Split 4 | The right hand alternates between floor tom and hi-hat.    **Track 67**

R L L R R L R L R L R R L R R L

The following example, **Groove 4 – Split 5**, shows a two-bar Split groove.

The right hand alternates back and forth between the hi-hat and ride cymbal. In this groove, you will automatically land on the ride cymbal on the first beat of measure 2.

Split grooves with hi-hat and ride cymbal:

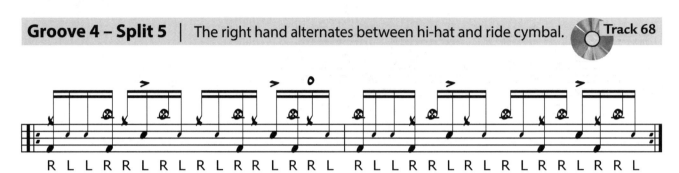

Groove 4 – Split 5 | The right hand alternates between hi-hat and ride cymbal. Track 68

Groove 4 – Split 6 | The right hand alternates between hi-hat and floor tom. Track 69

The examples **Groove 4 – Split 7** and **Groove 4 – Split 8** show two-bar Split grooves, in which the Split only appears briefly and, unlike before, does not always begin on the first beat.

Split grooves with hi-hat and ride cymbal:

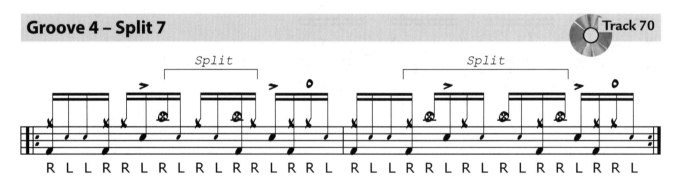

Groove 4 – Split 7 Track 70

Split grooves with hi-hat and floor tom:

Groove 4 – Split 8 Track 71

Step 6: The Switch

The hands change instruments: the right hand plays snare in the Switch and the left hand hi-hat. The sticking remains unchanged.

Groove 4 – Switch 1 | First you play the pattern without the accents on the snare.

Groove 4 – Switch 2 | Now with snare accents (here, on **2+**, **3a**, and **4+**).

Track 72

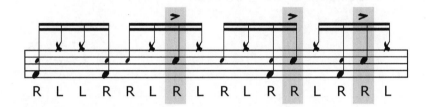

Once you have become accustomed to the Switch groove with accents, you should practice playing this groove alternately in customary fashion (right hand plays hi-hat) and as a Switch groove.

Groove 4 – Switch 3   Track 73

Measure 1: RH = hi-hat
Measure 2: RH = snare

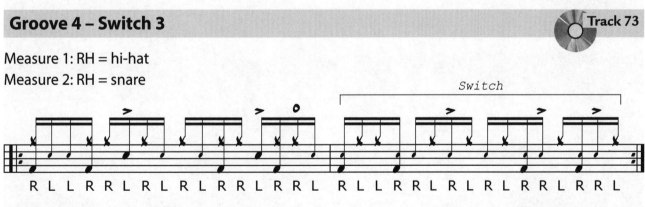

Groove 4 – Switch 4   Track 74

Measure 1: RH = snare
Measure 2: RH = hi-hat

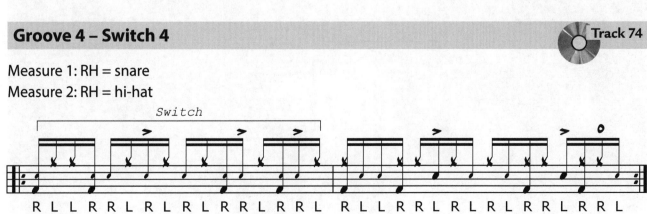

We will finish by playing one-bar Switch grooves. In the first half of the measure, the right hand plays the hi-hat and the left hand the snare.

Change hands on the third beat; the right hand plays the snare and the left hand the hi-hat.

Groove 4 – Switch 5

Track 75

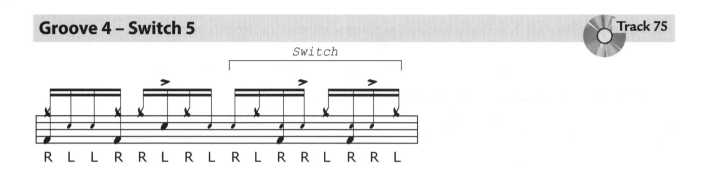

In the last groove in this chapter, you also change hands on the third beat.

Groove 4 – Switch 6

Track 76
Track 77

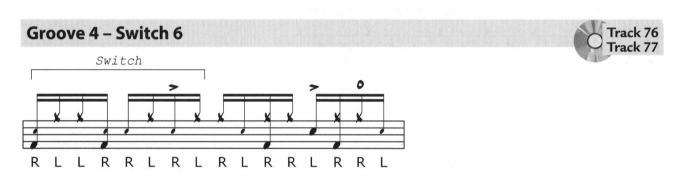

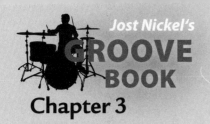

Chapter 3

Do It Yourself

In this chapter, I will show you how the grooves that I presented in *Chapter 2* originate.

We always start with a basic framework consisting of a bass drum pattern and snare accents, which is complemented step by step with ghost notes and a hi-hat pattern. The combination of bass drum and snare remains unchanged throughout all variations.

Example 1 – Initial Pattern (m. 3 from Reading Text 2)

1 e + a 2 e + a 3 e + a 4 e + a

The Four Basic Rules:

For the creation of grooves with intermittent/interrupted sixteenth notes, I utilize the following four rules systematically:

Rule 1: **The right hand begins on the first beat.**

Example – Rule 1

Rule 2: **The right hand plays on the sixteenth notes immediately before and after the snare accents.**

Example – Rule 2

Rule 3: **The right hand plays a maximum of two consecutive strokes.**

Rule 4: **The left hand plays exclusively single strokes.**

The application of these four rules can produce a variety of results. Below I will show you the creation process with two different versions of the groove.

If you apply *rules 3* and *4*, you can either play a ghost note with the left hand (*left column*) or a hi-hat beat with the right hand (*right column*) on **1e**.

Example 1 – Version 1.1

Example 1 – Version 2.1

Example 1 – Version 1.2

As the left hand only plays single strokes according to *rule 4*, the hi-hat follows on **1+**.

Example 1 – Version 2.2

As the right hand never plays more than two consecutive strokes according to *rule 3*, a ghost note follows on **1+**.

Example 1 – Version 1.3

On **1a**, you can now either play the hi-hat or a ghost note. To avoid ending up with too many versions, the left column only shows the version with the ghost note on **1a**.

Example 1 – Version 2.3

As the left hand only plays single strokes according to *rule 4*, the hi-hat follows on **1a**.

Example 1 – Version 1.4

As the left hand only plays single strokes according to *rule 4*, the hi-hat follows on **2**.

Example 1 – Version 2.4

According to *rule 3* the right hand never plays more than two consecutive strokes; a ghost note follows on **2**.

If you apply *rules 3* and *4*, you can either play a hi-hat beat with the right hand (*left column*) or a ghost note with the left hand on 3 (*right column*).

## Example 1 – Version 1.5	## Example 1 – Version 2.5

## Example 1 – Version 1.6	## Example 1 – Version 2.6

As the right hand never plays more than two consecutive strokes according to *rule 3*, a ghost note follows on **3e**.

As the left hand only plays single strokes according to *rule 4*, the hi-hat follows on **3e**.

## Example 1 – Version 1.7	## Example 1 – Version 2.7

As the left hand only plays single strokes according to *rule 4*, the hi-hat follows on **3+**.

A ghost note must follow on **3+** as the right hand never plays more than two consecutive strokes (*rule 3*).

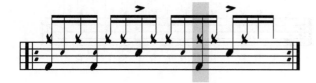 

If you are adhering to *rules 3* and *4*, you can either play a ghost note with the left hand (*left column*) or a hi-hat beat with the right hand (*right column*) on **4+**.

Example 1 – Version 1.8

Example 1 – Version 2.8

Example 1 – Version 1.9    Track 78

As the left hand only plays single strokes according to *rule 4*, the hi-hat follows on **4a**.

R L R L R R L R R L R R L R L R

Example 1 – Version 2.9    Track 79

A ghost note must follow on **4a** as the right hand never plays more than two consecutive strokes (*rule 3*).

R R L R L R L R L R L R L R R L

Here are two further versions of the groove that could have been developed from the described approach:

Example 1 – Version 3   Track 80

R L R R L R L R R L R R L R L R

Example 1 – Version 4   Track 81

R L R R L R L R L R L R L R R L

No Rule Without Exceptions

Breaking rules in music has never done any harm; on the contrary, it has always led to new developments!

As you have probably already noticed, the grooves in this chapter have up until now only contained single strokes in the left hand in adherence to *rule 4*.

If, however, I want to play a few occasional extra strokes in the left hand, this is what I do:

I substitute some of the single hi-hat beats with ghost notes. Here I ensure that neither of the two hands plays more than two consecutive strokes in the resulting groove.

Example 1A = Example 1 – Version 1.9 (*see p. 36*)

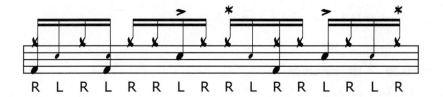

* = Hi-hat beats are substituted
by ghost notes.

Example 1B – Variation 1

Track 82

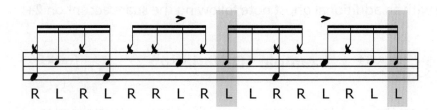

In the following groove, I have incorporated the ghost notes on **3** and **4a** in the original groove (the left and right hands play simultaneously on **3** and **4a**). According to my experience, this is harder to play than when the ghost notes appear on their own, but it sounds good!

Example 1C – Variation 2

Track 83

Now Rule 2 Bites the Dust

To recall *rule 2: the right hand plays on the sixteenth note immediately before and after the snare accents!*

This means that **rule 2** prevents ghost notes from being played before and after snare accents. At the beginning, this makes sense because it makes the grooves easier to play.

It is already technically demanding to play ghost notes directly after snare accents, but it is even harder to play ghost notes before snare accents, although both sound good!

➡ That means **rule 2** bites the dust now!

Nevertheless, continue to ensure that neither hand plays more than two consecutive strokes at a time.

To recall, here is the original groove:

Example 1D | Original Groove (*see Example 1 – Version 1.9 on p. 36*)

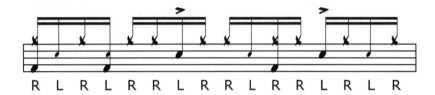

Here are two versions of our groove with an additional ghost note following the snare accent on **2+**:

Example 1D–Variation 1  Track 84	**Example 1D–Variation 2**  Track 85
In the *left column*, the ghost note *replaces* the hi-hat on **2a**.	In the *right column*, the ghost note is *added* to the groove on **2a**.

And another two versions with a ghost note before the snare accent on the **fourth beat**:

Example 1D–Variation 3 Track 86	**Example 1D–Variation 4** Track 87

My Recommendation:

After now having jettisoned almost all the rules, here is my suggestion:

It is imperative that you adhere to rules 1–4 for a certain time to discover good patterns.

You are justified in asking: How long is "for a certain time?"

My answer: A "certain time" lasts as long as you have the feeling that you are creating good grooves and are not becoming bored. After that, you are free to break all the rules!

You will find additional bass drum and snare combinations in the accompanying **Reading Texts 1** and **2**, which you can utilize to develop your own grooves based on *rules 1–4*.

In my early days, I noted down grooves on manuscript paper and tried them out on set. This process of experimentation will develop your feeling for recognizing which combinations you especially like. Also incorporate the Split and the Switch into your own grooves.

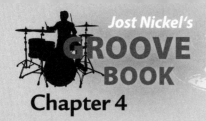
Linear Grooves

Grooves are termed linear if only played on a single instrument. This creates a special playing experience.

We will take **Example 1 from Reading Text 1** (just like at the beginning of *Chapter 2, page 12*).

Linear Groove – Initial Pattern   (Reading Text 1 – Example 1)

1 e + a 2 e + a 3 e + a 4 e + a

The example **Linear Groove 1** shows a way of filling in gaps in the **Linear Groove – Initial Pattern** with hi-hat beats and ghost notes.

Linear Groove 1

Track 88

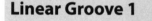

F L R R L R L F R L F R L R R L

F = foot

The next two variations illustrate two different options for modifying linear grooves.

Option 1: The **doubling** of single strokes sounds good in linear grooves. One sixteenth note is transformed into two thirty-second notes.

Linear Groove 1 – Variation 1

Track 89

F L R R L R L F R L F R L R R L

* = notes to be doubled

F L R R L R R L L F R R L L F R L R R L

* = notes have been doubled

Option 2: Now we employ the left foot. For this purpose, I divide all double strokes on the hi-hat: I play the first of the two double strokes with the left foot and the second with the right hand.

Linear Groove 1 – Variation 2

Track 90

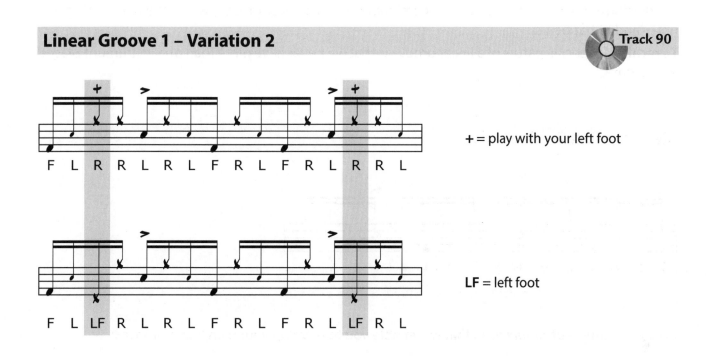

+ = play with your left foot

LF = left foot

The following two-bar linear grooves are combinations from the previously described grooves and groove ornamentation in this chapter.

Linear Groove 1 – Combination 1

Track 91

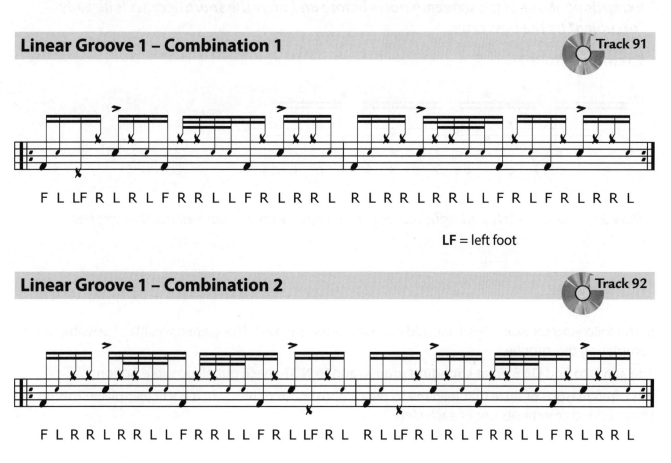

LF = left foot

Linear Groove 1 – Combination 2

Track 92

Do It Yourself

Your next task is to develop your own linear grooves. Here I also begin with a bass drum and snare combination. We will take **Example 3** from **Reading Text 2**.

To transform this bass drum and snare combination into a linear groove, we fill the gaps with ghost notes and hi-hat beats.

To recall, the special feature of a linear groove is that we never have more than one instrument played at one time.

Reading Text 2 – Example 3

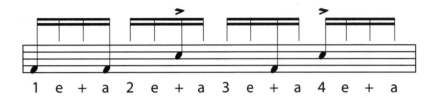

1 e + a 2 e + a 3 e + a 4 e + a

Here are a *couple of simple rules* that will enable you to develop your own linear grooves:

Two Simple Rules:

Rule 1: **The right hand plays on the sixteenth notes before and after the snare accents.**

Exception: **If one of the sixteenth notes before and after the snare accents is already "occupied" by the bass drum.**

Example – Rule 1

1 e + de 2 e + de 3 e + de 4 e + de

Rule 2: **Both the left and right hands play a maximum of two consecutive strokes.**

In the following six examples, I will add one beat after the next. There are a wealth of possibilities for completing this groove.

The aim is to find **ONE great sounding groove** and to **NOT** check out all possible options.

It is often reasons of taste that lead me to play a ghost note or hi-hat in a particular place. This is why I have added comments under each step.

Linear Groove A

1e: Ghost note or hi-hat?
If the first hi-hat beat of a groove comes on **1e**, this is unexpected and therefore a more special feature.
A less special variant would be to begin with a ghost note on **1e**, and not play the hi-hat until **1+**.

Linear Groove B

1+: Ghost note or hi-hat?
A ghost note follows on **1+**, because I like when hi-hat and ghost notes follow each other in linear grooves.

Linear Groove C

2: Ghost note or hi-hat?
Here we play a ghost note, so that the hi-hat can play **2e** after playing **1e**, thereby producing a repeating motif.

Linear Groove D

3 and 3e: Ghost notes
Play ghost notes on 3 and 3e ghost notes, so that we have double strokes on the snare in this groove.

Linear Groove E

4+: Hi-hat
On 4+ I play the hi-hat, so that we have a double stroke on the hi-hat in our groove.

Linear Groove F

F R L F L R L R L L F R L R R L

4a: Rule 2
On 4a rule 2 *comes into effect* with a maximum of two beats per hand: i.e. here we have a ghost note.

I am aware that the creation of this groove is highly dependent on individual taste. Do not be put off by the fact that there are so many different possibilities.

Rules 1 and *2* serve the purpose of simplifying the initial steps of creating linear grooves.

As soon as you start missing ghost notes directly before the snare accents, you should jettison *rule 1*. You can of course just as easily ignore **rule 2** and play more than two consecutive strokes with one hand.

In the accompanying **Reading Texts 1** and **2**, you will find further bass drum and snare combinations for developing your own linear grooves in accordance to *rules 1* and *2*.

In **Reading Text 1**, the snare is always accented on **2** and **4**.

From **Reading Text 2**, linear grooves can be developed with the snare accents on other beats.

When developing your own linear grooves, you should make copies of **Reading Texts 1** and **2** to enable you to note down your own ideas on these copies.

We will now double single strokes from **Linear Groove F** (*see page 44*) and also incorporate the left foot on the hi-hat as described at the beginning of this chapter.

All notes to be doubled are marked with an ✳.

All notes to be played with the left foot are marked with a ✛.

Linear Groove Study 1

(1)

F RR LL F   L R L   R   L L F R L R   R   L

(2)

F R L F   LL RR L R L L F R L R   R   L

(3)

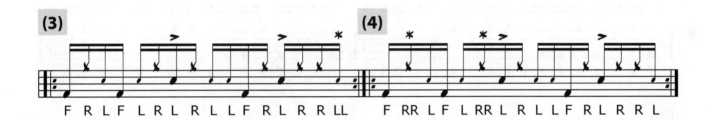

F R L F   L R L   R L L F R L R   R   LL

(4)

F RR L F   L RR L R L L F R L R   R   L

(5)

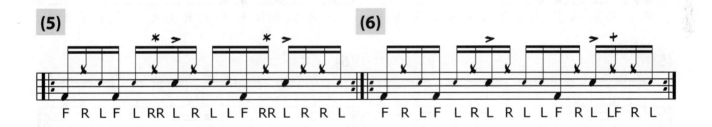

F R L F   L RR L   R L L F RR L R   R   L

(6)

F R L F   L R L   R L L F R L LF R   L

(7)

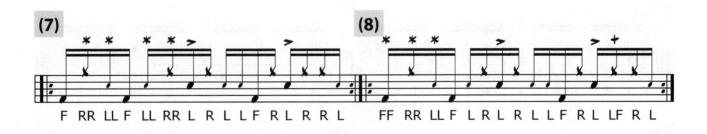

F RR LL F   LL RR L   R L L F R L R   R   L

(8)

FF RR LL F   L R L   R L L F R L LF R   L

✳ = *notes to be doubled*   ✛ = *play with left foot*

Linear Groove Study 2

Linear Groove Study 2 is entirely based on **Example 7** from **Reading Text 2**:

1   e   +   a   2   e   +   a   3   e   +   a   4   e   +   a

This pattern always remains constant in the following exercise. The grooves are distinguished from one another by the way in which the gaps are filled with ghost notes and hi-hat beats.

Note:

It is much easier if no ghost notes are played immediately *before and after* the snare accents. During the progress of this exercise, ghost notes occur *after* the snare accents from **No. 6** onwards. From **No. 9** onwards, ghost notes also occur *before* the snare accents.

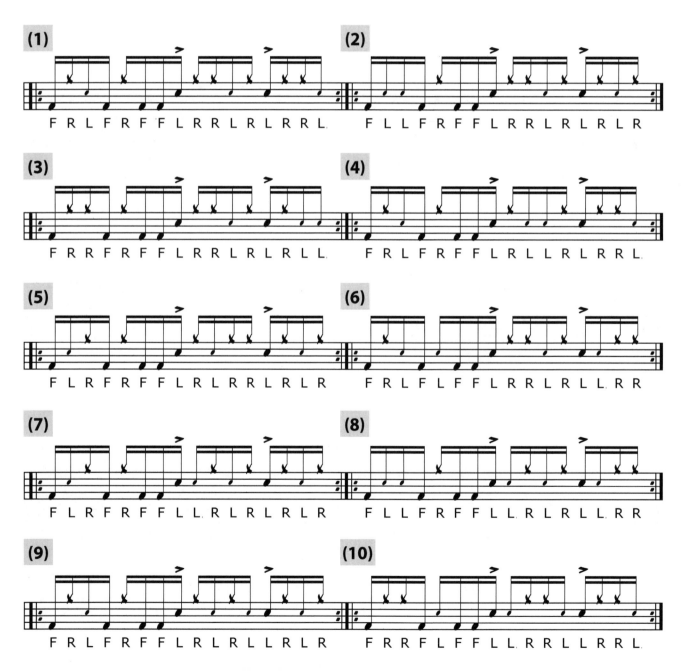

Linear Switch Grooves

Finally, I would also like to remind you that you can utilize the orchestration concept the Switch (*see chapter 2, pages 16–17*) for linear grooves.

When utilizing the Switch, the sticking remains unchanged, but the right hand plays the snare while the left hand plays the hi-hat.

Here is a linear groove based on **Reading Text 2 – Example 1**.

Initial Pattern: Reading Text 2 – Example 1

Linear Groove 2

The following groove is the Switch groove. The sticking remains unchanged, but the right hand plays the snare and the left hand the hi-hat.

Linear Switch Groove 1

Now we will alternate back and forth between the Switch groove and the original groove.

Linear Switch Groove 2

Measure 1 = right hand on the hi-hat
Measure 2 = right hand on the snare (The Switch)

Linear Switch Groove 3

Measure 1 = right hand on the snare (The Switch)
Measure 2 = right hand on the hi-hat

Now we come to the single-bar versions of the Switch. In the first half of the bar, the right hand plays the hi-hat and the left hand the snare. The hands are swapped on **3e**.

Linear Switch Groove 4

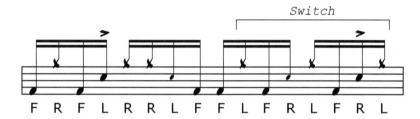

In the first half of the measure, the right hand plays the snare and the left hand the hi-hat. The hands are swapped on **3e**.

Linear Switch Groove 5

Summary

Linear grooves are characterized by each instrument standing alone.

1. We have altered linear grooves by doubling single strokes and the division of hi-hat double strokes between the left foot and the right hand.

2. You can think out your own linear grooves by adhering to *two rules*.

Rule 1 = Right hand plays before and after the snare accents.

Rule 2 = Right hand and left hand play a maximum of two consecutive strokes.

3. The orchestration concept the Switch can also be utilized in linear grooves.

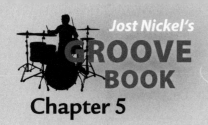
Ghost Notes

I use **two different approaches** to ghost notes.

1. Ostinato Approach [*Ital.: ostinato = persistent*] *– an ostinato is a constantly recurring repeated figure:*

In the Ostinato Approach, you play a ghost note ostinato, which remains unchanged independently of the hi-hat and bass drum pattern.

2. Intertwined Approach:

The Intertwined Approach is the second method of playing ghost notes. Here the ghost note pattern is dependent on the bass drum pattern. The bass drum pattern and the ghost notes are interlocked with each other.

Ghost Notes 1 – Ostinato Approach

Ghost Note Ostinato 1

RH = hi-hat
LH = snare

This pattern remains constant irrespective of what the bass drum plays along with it. Here we focus on adding bass drum patterns. This is achieved in three steps of ascending difficulty. We begin with bass drum patterns in eighth notes.

Here you take **Reading Text 3 – Quarter and Eighth Notes** and play this with the bass drum and **Ghost Note Ostinato 1 (GO1)**.

The first level of difficulty is **Ghost Note Ostinato 1 (GO 1)** with **Reading Text 3 – Quarter and Eighth Notes**.

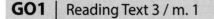
GO1 | Reading Text 3 / m. 1

Track 100

Practice Tip: There are different methods of practicing with the reading texts.

1. Play one-bar grooves. As an example, repeat measure 1 of the reading text eight times, then repeat measure 2 eight times and so on.

2. Play two-bar grooves. Simply select two consecutive bars from the reading text and repeat these:

Ghost Note Ostinato 1 plus Reading Text 3, measures 2 and 3

3. Play the entire reading text without repeats from measure 1 to the end.

In concrete terms, this means that you begin as described in step 1.

If this works well, after some time (one week, for example), you can progress to practicing as described in step 2.

Finally, you can progress to practicing as described in step 3.

The second level of difficulty is **Ghost Note Ostinato 1 (GO 1)** with **Reading Text 4 – 16ths (1)**.

Here are measures 1–4 from **Reading Text 4** in the bass drum:

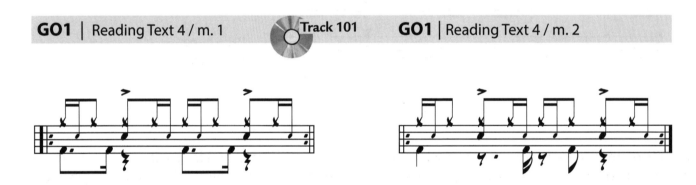

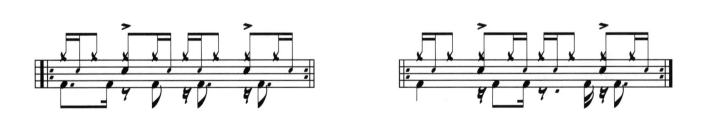

I also recommend playing one- and two-bar grooves with the second level of difficulty.

The third level of difficulty is **Ghost Note Ostinato 1 (GO 1)** plus **Reading Text 5 16ths (2)**. Here are measures 1–4 from **Reading Text 5** in the bass drum:

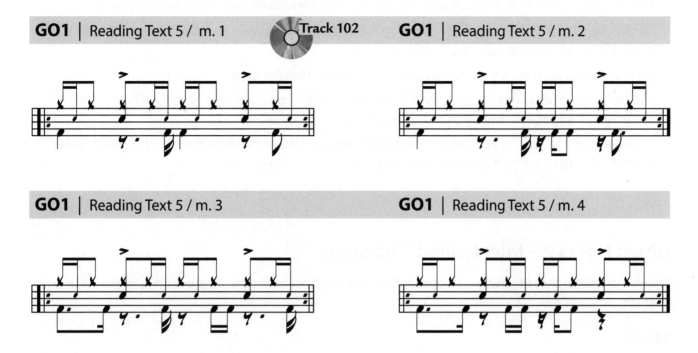

Here it is also a good idea to play both one- and two-bar grooves.

Now we follow up with six **Ghost Note Ostinatos** (you are already familiar with the first one), which you can all play with **Reading Texts 3, 4,** and **5**.

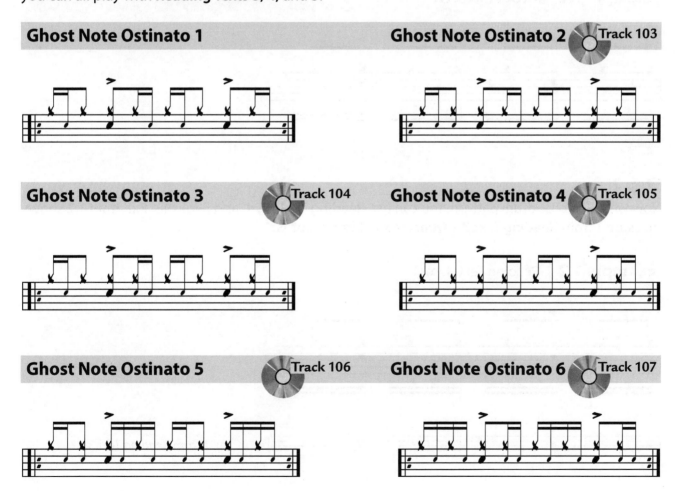

Practice Tip: As there are so many possibilities in the combination of the reading texts and all six ghost note ostinatos, you can easily lose your way and spend too much time on them.

I recommend that you practice for about 20 minutes a day on your ghost notes, and during this time, alternate between one- and two-bar grooves.

It is also not necessary to practice all ghost note ostinatos one after the other.

On the contrary, after having practiced **Ghost Note Ostinato 1**, it is better to continue with **Ghost Notes 2 – Intertwined Approach** (*see below*).

Once you have practiced your way through this volume, you can come back to the ghost notes or return to this practice book at a later time.

Ghost Notes 2 – Intertwined Approach

Now we come to the **Intertwined Approach,** in which ghost notes are interlinked with the bass drum pattern.

Step 1:

First you need a hi-hat pattern and snare accents. The basis for our groove is eighth notes on the hi-hat and snare accents on **2** and **4**.

Example 1.1 – Initial Pattern

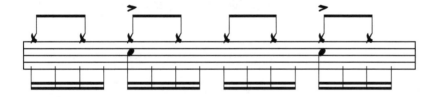

Step 2:

Now we add a bass drum pattern. You can use **Reading Texts 3, 4,** and **5** for this. **Example 1.2** shows measure 1 from **Reading Text 3 – Quarter and Eighth Notes**.

Example 1.2 | Reading Text 3 /m. 1

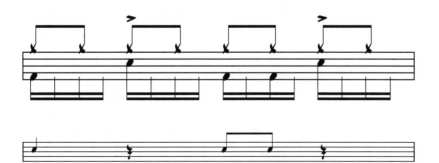

m. 1 from Reading Text 3

Step 3:

You play ghost notes on ALL remaining sixteenth notes.

Example 1.3 | Reading Text 3 / m. 1

In slower tempos (quarter note = 60–85), it naturally sounds good when you play all ghost notes (**Example 1.3**). This is additionally a good exercise for the left hand.

For faster tempos, you should omit the ghost notes as described in **Step 4** below.

Step 4:

For better playability, particularly in faster tempos, all ghost notes directly before and after the snare accents are initially omitted. Secondly, you do not play more than two consecutive strokes in the left hand.

Example 1.4 | Reading Text 3 / m. 1

Four-Step Ghost Note Concept:

Summary of the four steps to playing intertwined ghost note grooves:

Step 1: Hi-hat pattern plus snare accents

Step 2: Bass drum pattern from Reading Texts 3, 4, and 5

Step 3: Ghost notes on all remaining sixteenth notes

Step 4: Omit ghost notes before and after snare accents (the left hand does not play more than two consecutive strokes).

Video-Trailer

This QR Code will lead you to a video about Ghost Notes.

We will now utilize these **four steps** as an example using extracts from **Reading Texts 4, 5, and 2.**

Step 1: Eighth notes on the hi-hat with **2** and **4** on the snare.

Example 2.1 – Initial Pattern

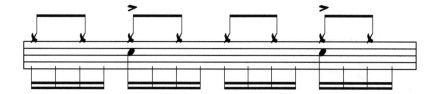

Step 2: An example with sixteenth notes in the bass drum.

Example 2.2 | Reading Text 4 / m. 1

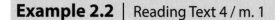
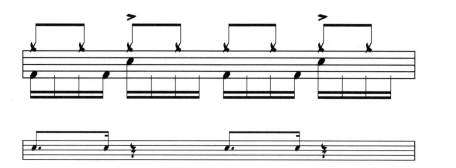

m. 1 from Reading Text 4

Step 3: Play ghost notes on all remaining sixteenth notes.

Example 2.3 | Reading Text 4 / m. 1

Step 4: Omit ghost notes before and after snare accents.
(The left hand does not play more than two consecutive strokes.)

Example 2.4 | Reading Text 4 / m. 1

Track 110

Step 1: Eighth notes on the hi-hat with 2 and 4 on the snare.

Example 3.1 – Initial Pattern

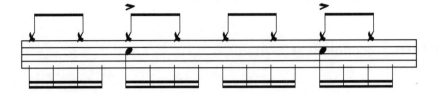

Step 2: An example with sixteenth notes in the bass drum.

Example 3.2 | Reading Text 5 / Measure 1

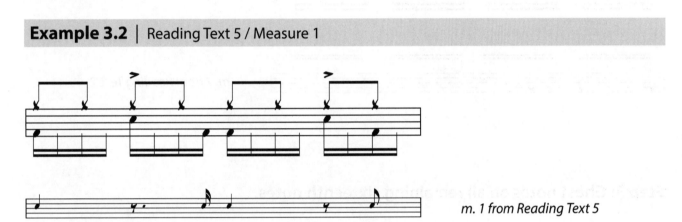

m. 1 from Reading Text 5

Step 3: Ghost notes on all remaining sixteenth notes.

Example 3.3 | Reading Text 5 / m. 1

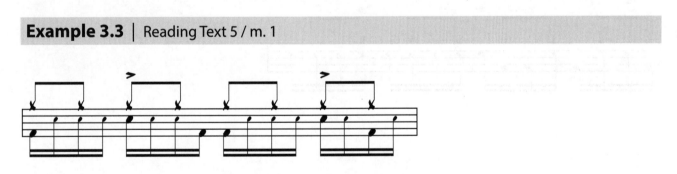

**Step 4: Omit ghost notes before and after snare accents.
(The left hand does not play more than two consecutive strokes.)**

Example 3.4 | Reading Text 5 / m. 1   🔘 Track 111

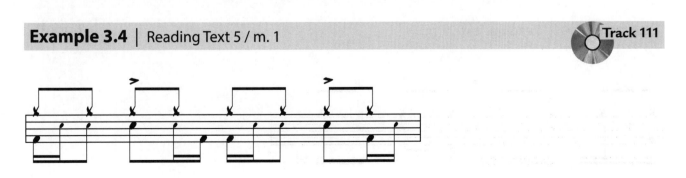

Now we will take an eighth-note hi-hat plus measure 7 from **Reading Text 2 – Bass Drum and Snare (2)**. If we use this reading text, we can create grooves with snare accents on other parts of the beat than on **2** and **4**.

We therefore already have our hi-hat and snare pattern (**Step 1**) and the bass drum pattern (**Step 2**):

Example 4.1 / 4.2 – Initial Pattern | Reading Text 2 / m. 7

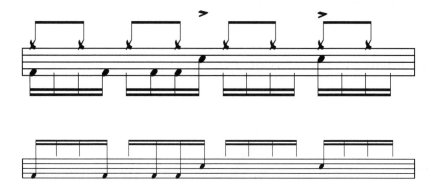

m. 7 from Reading Text 2

Step 3: Ghost notes on all remaining sixteenth notes.

Example 4.3 | Reading Text 2 / m. 7

Step 4: Omit ghost notes before and after snare accents.
(The left hand does not play more than two consecutive strokes.)

Example 4.4 | Reading Text 2 / m. 7

Track 112

Ghost Notes 3 – Ghost Notes Before and After Snare Accents

You can NATURALLY also play ghost notes before and after snare accents. For this purpose, we will now add ghost notes before and after snare accents to the grooves, which have evolved from **Reading Texts 3, 4, 5,** and **2.**

The first of these grooves was **Example 1.4** on the basis of **Reading Text 3** (*see page 53*).

To recall, here is **Example 1.4** again:

Example 1.4   Track 109

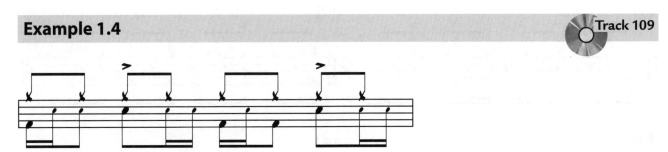

Now we will play ghost notes after the snare accents on **2** and **4**. The left hand continues to play a maximum of two consecutive strokes.

Example 1.4 – Variation 1 (ghost notes **after** snare accents)   Track 113

We will now play ghost notes before the snare accents on **2** and **4**. The left hand continues to play a **maximum of two consecutive strokes.**

Example 1.4 – Variation 2 (ghost notes **before** snare accents)   Track 114

Finally, we come to our supreme challenge; we now play **more than two consecutive strokes** in the left hand. We play ghost notes **before and after** the snare accents on **2** and **4.**

Example 1.4 – Variation 3 (ghost notes **before and after** snare accents)   Track 115

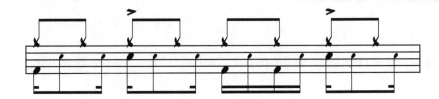

Ghost Note Study 1

After having practiced the four different ghost note patterns in **Example 1.4**, you should now practice the different grooves consecutively. The bass drum pattern, snare accents, and hi-hat pattern remain unchanged, and it is only the ghost notes that are altered. Repeat each groove four or eight times.

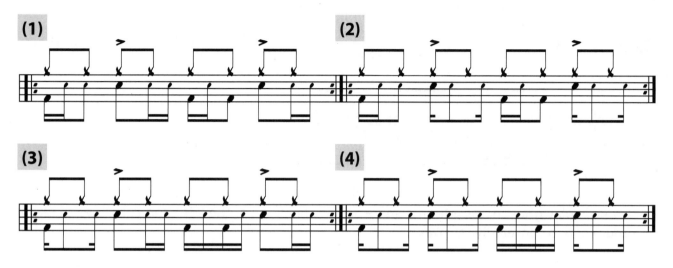

Let us now return to **Example 2.4** (*see page 54*) on the basis of **Reading Text 4** and add ghost notes. **To recall**, here is Example 2.4 again:

Example 2.4   Track 110

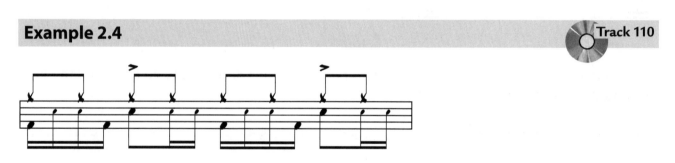

We will now play ghost notes **after** the snare accents on **2** and **4**. The left hand continues to play a **maximum of two consecutive strokes**.

Example 2.4 – Variation 1 (ghost notes **after** snare accents)   Track 116

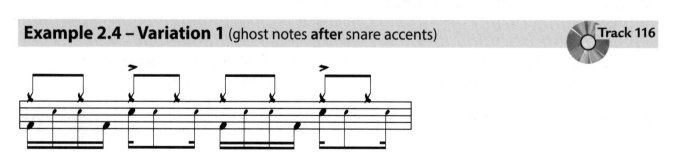

We do not play ghost notes **before** the snare accents in this groove as the bass drum is already playing on these beats.

Let us return to **Example 3.4** (*see page 55*) on the basis of **Reading Text 4** and add ghost notes.
To recall, here is Example 3.4 again:

Example 3.4

Now we play ghost notes **after** the snare accents on **2** and **4**. The left hand continues to play a **maximum of two consecutive strokes**.

Example 3.4 – Variation 1 (ghost notes **after** snare accents)

Now we play ghost notes **before** the snare accents on **2** and **4**. The left hand continues to play a **maximum of two consecutive strokes**.

Example 3.4 – Variation 2 (ghost notes **before** snare accents)

We finally come again to the **supreme challenge**:
We now play ghost notes **before and after** the snare accents on **2** and **4**:

Example 3.4 – Variation 3 (ghost notes **before and after** snare accents)

Ghost Note Study 2

Here are the four versions of **Example 3.4**. The bass drum pattern, snare accents, and hi-hat pattern remain unchanged, and it is only the ghost notes that are altered.

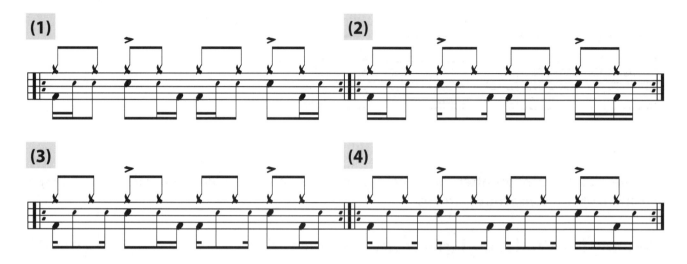

Practice Tip: Continue playing the groove until it feels natural and like the easiest thing in the world. Generally, I recommend that you think in measure blocks of four, eight, or sixteen.

Let us return to **Example 4.4** (*see page 56*) on the basis of **Reading Text 4** and add ghost notes.

To recall, here is Example 4.4 again:

Example 4.4

As in the previous grooves, there are ghost notes **after** the snare accents.

Example 4.4 – Variation 1 (ghost notes **after** snare accents)

Now we transform **Example 4.4** into a groove with a ghost note before the snare accent on **4.**

We do not play a ghost note on **2a**, as the bass drum is already playing here. The left hand continues to play a **maximum of two consecutive strokes.**

Example 4.4 – Variation 2 (ghost notes **before** snare accents)

Here is a groove with ghost notes **before and after** the snare accent on **4.**

Example 4.4 – Variation 3 (ghost notes **before and after** snare accents)

Now we come to a series of ten different versions of **Example 4.4** containing all ghost note concepts covered in this chapter.

The bass drum pattern, snare accents, and hi-hat pattern remain unchanged, and it is only the ghost notes that are altered.

Repeat each groove until you feel good about it and relaxed while playing before progressing to the next one. Always think in measure blocks of four, eight, or sixteen.

Ghost Note Study 3

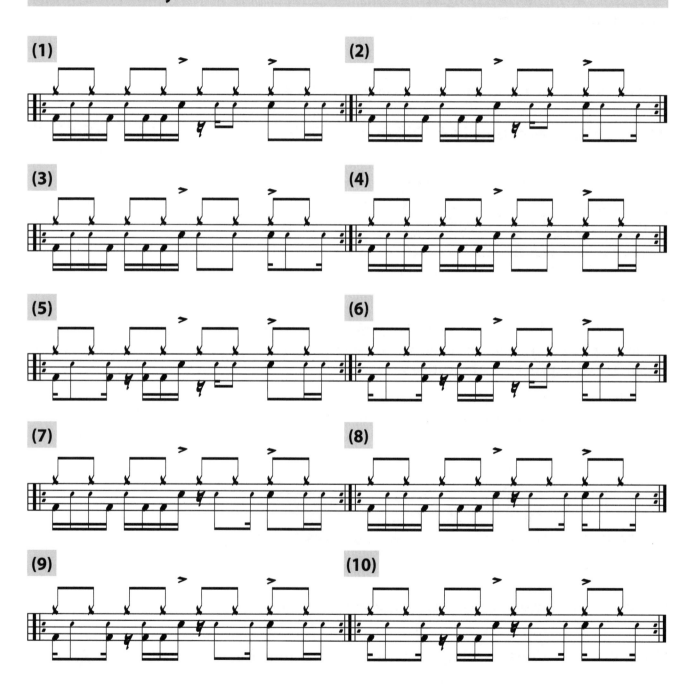

At the end of this chapter, we come to our free exercise: here are ten different ghost note grooves with changes in the bass drum and snare accents at different positions.

Once again: Practice each groove until you feel relaxed with it before progressing to the next one.

Ghost Note Study 4

Summary

We can play ghost notes in two different ways:

1. Ostinato Approach: The left hand plays a ghost note ostinato **independently** from the bass drum pattern. To practice this, we use **Reading Texts 3, 4,** and **5** as the bass drum pattern.

2. Intertwined Approach: The left hand plays a ghost note pattern **dependent** on the bass drum pattern. At the beginning, we do not play ghost notes before and after the snare accents so that the grooves do not present too many technical challenges at once.

In three further steps, we play ghost notes:

1. **after** snare accents,
2. **before** snare accents, and
3. **before and after** snare accents.

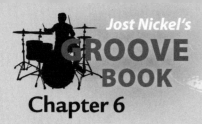

Bass Drum Displacement

In this chapter, we concentrate on **two different methods** of altering a bass drum part to transform a one-bar groove into a two-bar groove.

Displacement of a Bass Drum Beat

Two-bar grooves add greater variety to your part in a song. That is why it is good to get to know a few ways of developing two-bar grooves. We begin with the displacement of the bass drum beat.

Here we will utilize **Reading Texts 3, 4, 5,** and **2** in this volume. The level of difficulty ascends from one reading text to the next. I have notated the first measure of each reading text as an example, but you should always practice the whole of each single reading text.

We start with **Reading Text 3 (Quarter and Eighth Notes)**. The right hand plays eighth notes on the hi-hat, the left hand plays on the snare on **2** and **4**, and the bass drum plays **Measure 1** from **Reading Text 3**.

1. Reading Text 3 – Measure 1 (Initial Pattern)

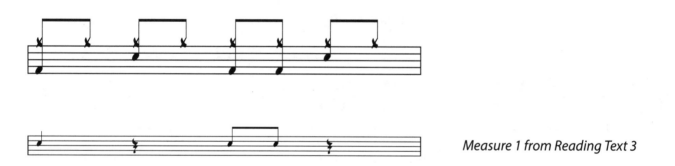

Measure 1 from Reading Text 3

To transform this into a two-bar pattern, we play the bass drum in the repeat **an eighth note earlier** than on the **first beat**, i.e. on **4+** of the first measure.

1A. BD Displacement 1

Track 133

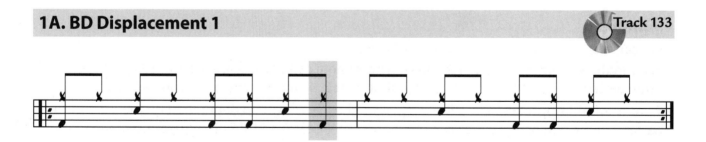

Another good alternative is to play the bass drum **an eighth note later** in the repeat. In the second measure, we therefore have the bass drum on **1+** instead of on **1**.

1B. BD Displacement 2

Track 134

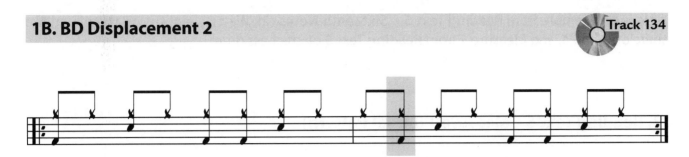

Generally, you must always check whether these two-bar grooves go well with the song you are playing. If you are in the process of composing or arranging a song, you can, for example, suggest that the bass player in your band synchronizes his bass pattern with your groove.

Now we come to an example from **Reading Text 4 – Sixteenth Notes (1)**. Again we play eighths on the hi-hat, on **2** and **4** on the snare, and **Measure 1** from **Reading Text 4** on the bass drum.

2. Reading Text 4 – Measure 1 (Initial Pattern)

Measure 1 from Reading Text 4

To turn this into a two-bar pattern, we play the bass drum in the repeat **a sixteenth note earlier,** i.e. on **4a** of the first measure.

2A. BD Displacement 1

Track 135

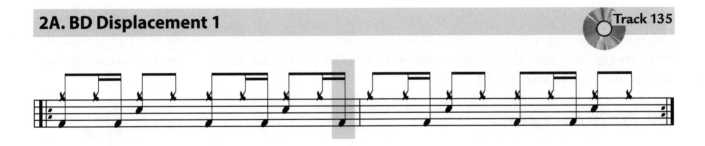

Now we play the bass drum **a sixteenth note later** in the repeat. In the second measure, the bass drum wanders from **1** to **1e**.

2B. BD Displacement 2

Track 136

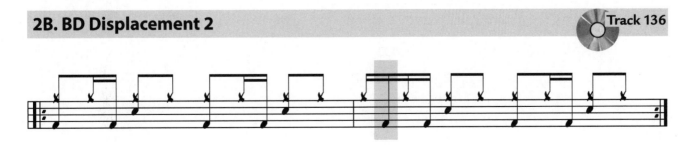

Here is an example from **Reading Text 5 – Sixteenth Notes** (2). We play eighths on the hi-hat, the snare on **2** and **4**, and **Measure 1** from **Reading Text 5** on the bass drum.

3. Reading Text 5 – Measure 1 (Initial Pattern)

Measure 1 from Reading Text 5

To transform this into a two-bar pattern, we play the bass drum in the repeat **a sixteenth note earlier**, i.e. on **4a** of the first measure.

3A. BD Displacement 1   Track 137

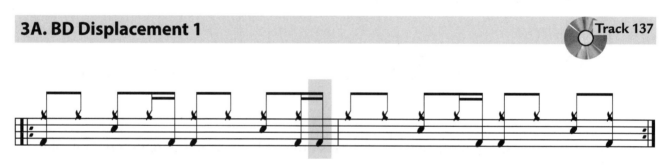

Now we play the bass drum a **sixteenth note later** in the repeat. In the second measure, the bass drum comes on **1e** instead of **1**.

3B. BD Displacement 2   Track 138

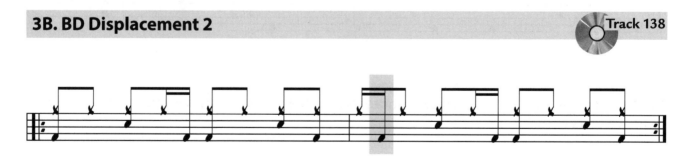

Now we turn to an example from **Reading Text 2 – Bass Drum and Snare (2)**. The special feature of this reading text is that it consists of bass drum and snare patterns.

We play **Measure 1** from **Reading Text 2** alongside eighth notes on the hi-hat. The snare plays accents on **1a** and **4**.

4. Reading Text 2 – Measure 1 (Initial Pattern)

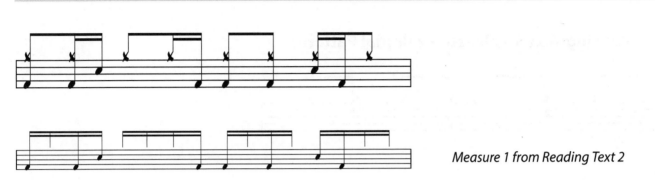

Measure 1 from Reading Text 2

To transform this into a two-bar pattern, we play the bass drum in the repeat on **1 a sixteenth note earlier**, i.e. on **4a** of the first measure.

4A. BD Displacement 1　　　　　　　　　　　　　　　　　Track 139

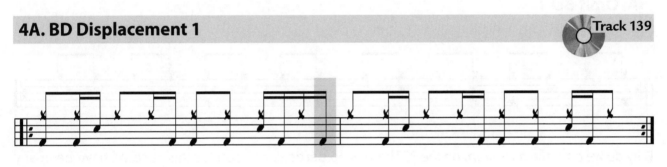

Now we play the bass drum **a sixteenth note later** in the repeat. In the second measure, the bass drum wanders from **1** to **1e**.

4B. BD Displacement 2　　　　　　　　　　　　　　　　　Track 140

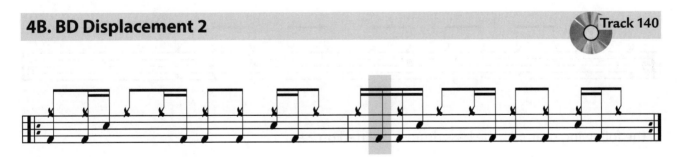

Omitting a Bass Drum Beat

It is also possible to turn a one-bar pattern into a two-bar pattern by omitting a beat.

We will practice this using **Reading Texts 3, 4, 5,** and **2.**

The right hand plays eighth notes on the hi-hat, the left hand plays the snare on **2** and **4,** and the bass drum plays **Measure 2** from **Reading Text 3 (Quarters and Eighth Notes).**

5. Reading Text 3 – Measure 2 (Initial Pattern)

Measure 2 from Reading Text 3

In measure 2, the bass drum is omitted on **3.** Here is the two-bar groove:

5A. Omit BD 1

Why do we omit the bass drum on the 3? There is no particular reason for this. It could have been any of the other bass drum beats from **Initial Pattern 5.** See what happens if you omit the bass drum on **1** instead of on **3** (**Example 5B**) or on **2+** (**Example 5C**). In measure 2 of the next example, the bass drum is omitted on **1.**

5B. Omit BD 2

In the following example, the bass drum is omitted on **2+.**

5C. Omit BD 3

It is not necessary to check out all possibilities in the following grooves. You are, however, now aware that if you want to use the omission of bass drum beats to create two-bar grooves within the context of a band, it is worth exploring the possibilities of different positions, as the effect is noticeably different depending on which beat is omitted.

Now we come to an example from **Reading Text 4 – Sixteenth Notes (1)**. Here we utilize the same principle: the hi-hat plays eighth notes, the snare plays on **2** and **4**, and the bass drum plays **Measure 2** from **Reading Text 4**.

6. Reading Text 4 – Measure 2 (Initial Pattern)

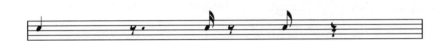

Measure 2 from Reading Text 4

In measure 2 the bass drum is omitted on **1**.

6A. Omit BD

Here is an example from **Reading Text 5 – Sixteenth Notes (2)**. As before, the hi-hat plays eighth notes, the snare plays on **2** and **4**, and the bass drum plays **Measure 2** from **Reading Text 5**.

7. Reading Text 5 – Measure 2 (Initial Pattern)

Measure 2 from Reading Text 5

In measure 2 the bass drum is omitted on **2a**.

7A. Omit BD

Now we come to an example from **Reading Text 2 – Bass Drum and Snare** (2). The special feature of this reading text is that it consists of bass drum and snare figures.

We play **Measure 2** from **Reading Text 2** alongside eighth notes on the hi-hat. The snare now plays accents on **2e** and **4**.

8. Reading Text 2 – Measure 2 (Initial Pattern)

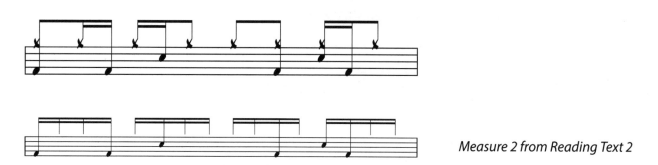

Measure 2 from Reading Text 2

In the repeat, the bass drum is omitted in the second measure on **1a**.

8A. Omit BD

Summary

We transform one-bar grooves into two-bar grooves and utilize **two different approaches**:

1. Displacement of the bass drum beat:
- In eighth-note grooves, the bass drum in measure 2 on the first beat is played **either an eighth note earlier or later**.
- In sixteenth-note grooves, the same procedure is followed in sixteenth notes. In the repeat, the bass drum at the beginning of measure 2 is played **either a sixteenth note earlier or later**.

2. Omitting a bass drum beat:
In measure 2, one bass drum beat of the original groove is omitted.

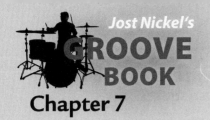

Snare Displacement

In this chapter, I will show you how to create new grooves by displacing snare beats.

Our skeleton groove consists of an eighth-note hi-hat and the snare on **2** and **4**. The bass drum patterns will be taken from the various reading texts in this book.

Example A shows the first measure from **Line 4** of **Reading Text 4 – Sixteenth Notes (1)** in the bass drum.

Reading Text 4 – Line 4 – Measure 1 in the Bass Drum (Initial Pattern)

Reading Text 4 – Line 4 – Measure 4

We systematically displace the snare from the second beat to different positions in the first half of the measure while the rest of the groove remains unchanged.

Snare Displacement Study 1

In measure (2) the snare comes on **1+** together with the bass drum. If snare and bass drum are to be played simultaneously, you can omit the bass drum. The same occurs in measure (4) on **2e**.

71

These grooves are crying out for ghost notes. Two things are necessary to find good ghost note patterns for the left hand that go well with all grooves with displaced snare strokes.

1. Play ghost notes on all sixteenth-note offbeats.
Here is an example with **Groove 1** from *Snare Displacement Study 1*:

Groove 1 (from: Snare Displacement Study 1)

1 e + a 2 e + a 3 e + a 4 e + a

2. Now we omit all ghost notes before and after the snare accents.
That means that the ghost notes on **3a** and **4e** are omitted in Groove 1.

The omitting of these ghost notes achieves a better playability. If you wish, however, you can play all the ghost notes ...

Omit Ghost Notes Before AND After the Snare Accents

Here again are all grooves from *Snare Displacement Study 1* with ghost notes.

Snare Displacement Study 2

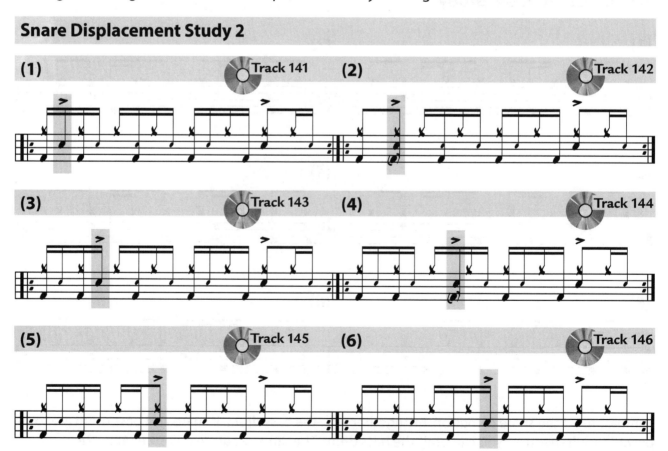

I use the displacement of snare strokes first to discover completely new grooves, which I play as one-bar patterns. Secondly, the displacement of the snare is also a good technique for developing two-bar patterns.

The following grooves are two-bar patterns consisting of the original groove (*Initial Pattern, p. 71*) and the grooves from *Snare Displacement Study 2*.

The original groove is also played with ghost notes:

Snare Displacement Study 3

(1)

(2)

(3)

(4)

(5)

Track 147

(6)

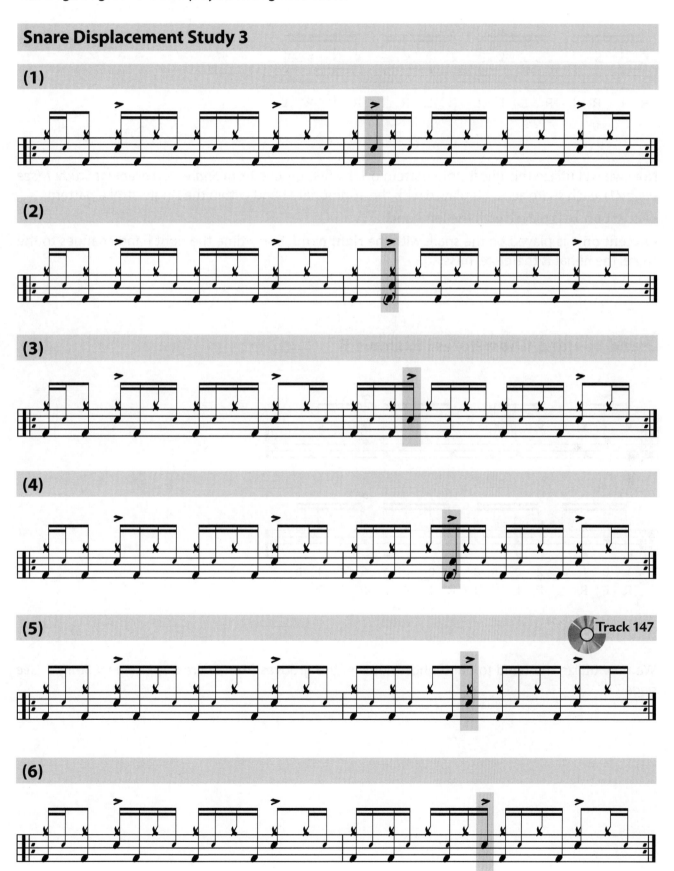

I must include a further ghost-note variant at this point. The hands play a sixteenth-note pattern consisting exclusively of *singles* (*single strokes = hand-to-hand*). The right hand plays the hi-hat and the left hand plays ghost notes on the snare.

Hand-to-Hand Ghost Notes – Initial Pattern

R   L   R   L   R   L   R   L   R   L   R   L   R   L   R   L

Now we will utilize this ghost note pattern on the first groove from *Snare Displacement Study 1* (*see page 71*): each snare accent is played with the appropriate hand within the single-stroke pattern:

• **Accent on 1e** is played with the **left hand.**

• **Accent on 4** is played on the snare with the **right hand**. Every time the right hand changes to the snare, the hi-hat is therefore "missing."

Hand-to-Hand Ghost Notes | Example B

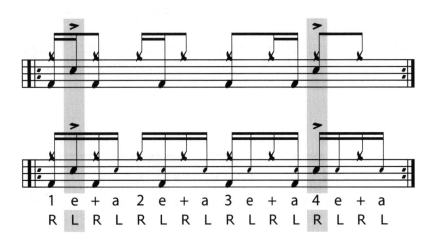

1   e   +   a   2   e   +   a   3   e   +   a   4   e   +   a
R   L   R   L   R   L   R   L   R   L   R   L   R   L   R   L

We now utilize the hand-to-hand ghost notes in the grooves from *Snare Displacement Study 1* (*see page 71*).

Snare Displacement Study 4 | Hand-to-Hand Ghost Notes

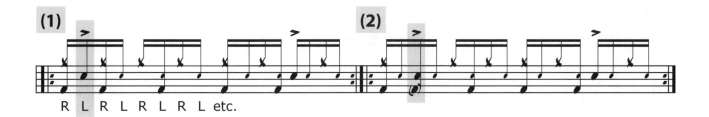

R L R L R L R L etc.

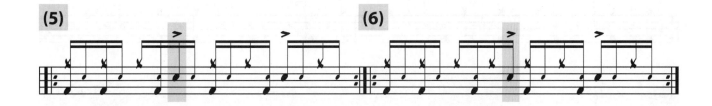

The following grooves are two-bar patterns taken from the original groove (*Initial Pattern, see p. 71*) and the grooves from *Snare Displacement Study 4*:

The original groove is now also played with hand-to-hand ghost notes.

Snare Displacement Study 5 | Hand-to-Hand Ghost Notes

(1)   Track 148

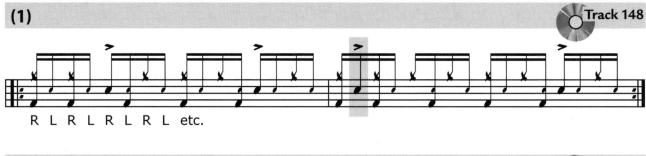

R L R L R L R L etc.

(2)   Track 149

(3)   Track 150

(4)   Track 151

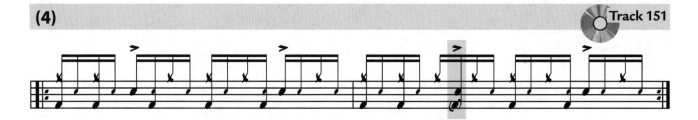

(5)   Track 152

(6)   Track 153

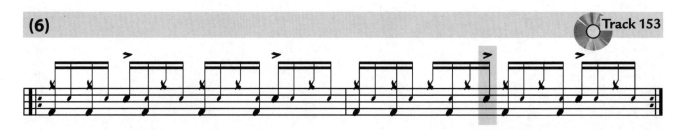

The attentive observer will surely have noticed that we have not yet displaced the snare on **4**: we cannot leave this stone unturned.

We therefore systematically displace the snare to different positions in the second half of the measure while the rest of the groove remains unchanged (the snare on **2** is not displaced in any of the following examples).

To recall, here is the original pattern (*see p. 71*):

Reading Text 4 – Line 4 – Measure 1 in the Bass Drum (Initial Pattern)

Now the snare on **4** is displaced.

Snare Displacement Study 6

(1)   **(2)**

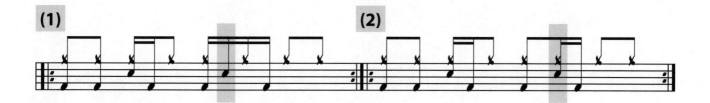

(3)   **(4)**

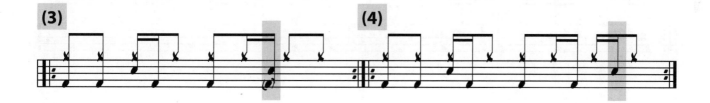

(5)   **(6)**

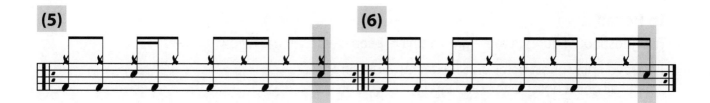

Here once again are all grooves from *Snare Displacement Study 6* with ghost notes:

Snare Displacement Study 7

(1) Track 154   **(2)** Track 155

(3) Track 156   **(4)** Track 157

(5) Track 158   **(6)** Track 159

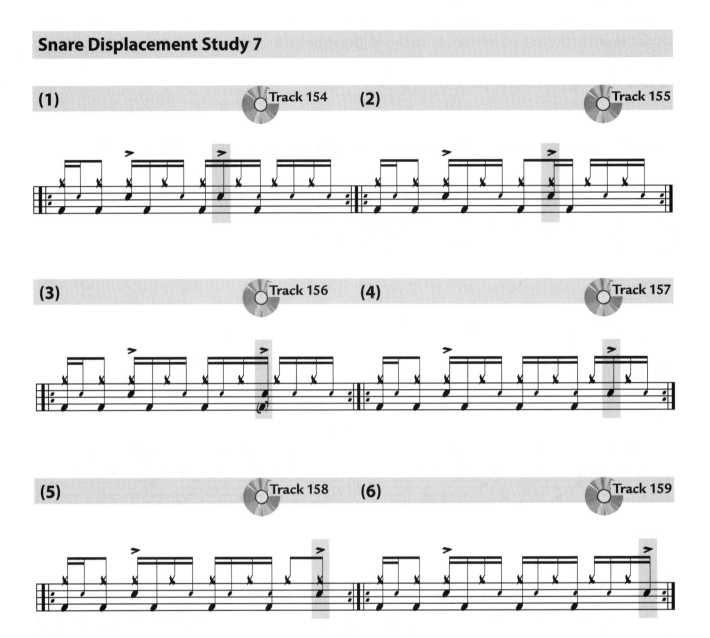

To Recall

The ghost note figures in these grooves have been created in the following ways:

1. First you play ghost notes on all sixteenth-note offbeats.
2. Omit all ghost notes before and after snare accents.

The following grooves are two-bar patterns consisting of the original groove (*Initial Pattern, see p. 71*) and the groove from *Snare Displacement Study 6* (*see p. 77*).

The original groove is now also played with ghost notes.

In the two-bar grooves from *Snare Displacement Study 3* (*see p. 73*), the original groove previously came first, whereas now for a change this always comes in measure 2.

Snare Displacement Study 8

Here are the grooves from *Snare Displacement Study 7* (*see p. 78*) with hand-to-hand ghost notes.

Snare Displacement Study 9 | Hand-to-Hand Ghost Notes

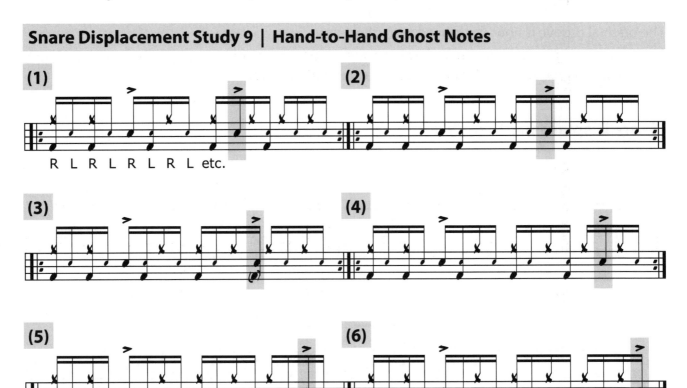

To Recall

The ghost note figures in these grooves have been created in the following ways:

• The hands play sixteenth notes as single strokes = *singles*.

• Right hand = hi-hat (all eighth notes).

• Left hand = ghost notes on the snare (all sixteenth-note offbeats).

Each snare accent is played with the appropriate hand from the single-stroke patterns. If one of the accents falls on the right hand, you play the snare with it and the hi-hat is automatically omitted.

The following grooves are two-bar patterns originating from the original groove (*Initial Pattern, see page 71*) and the grooves from *Snare Displacement Study 9*:

The original groove is now also played with hand-to-hand ghost notes.

Snare Displacement Study 10 | Hand-to-Hand Ghost Notes

R L R L R L R L etc.

All grooves in this chapter have the same bass drum pattern. If you are therefore interested in creating more grooves of this type, choose a different pattern and continue as described.

Summary

Starting with our basic skeleton groove consisting of hi-hat eighth notes, snare drum on **2** and **4**, and a bass drum pattern (**Reading Texts 4** or **5**), we create new one- or two-bar grooves.

We displace **one of the two snare accents** while the rest of the groove remains unchanged.

The snare on **2** is displaced within the first half of the measure and the snare on **4** in the second half of the measure:

1. Ghost note pattern in the left hand
2. Hand-to-hand ghost notes.

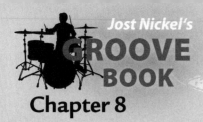

Chapter 8

Half Time – Double Time

In this chapter, we focus on different snare positions within the groove to alter the character of the groove. Depending on whether you play the snare on **2** and **4**, or only on **3**, or alternatively on all **and** beats, the groove will sound half or double as fast.

What we play here on the hi-hat or bass drum is not so important: the decisive factor is the **placing** of the snare accents.

All exercises are based on the same principle:

Hi-hat and bass drum patterns remain unchanged, and it is only the snare position that is changed.

Example 1A

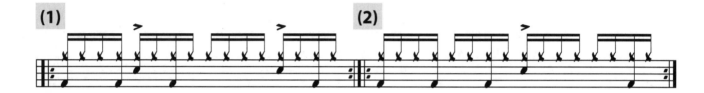

Measure (1) is the basic groove.

Measure (2) is the half-time version of the basic groove.

Measure (3) is the double-time version of the basic groove.

Measure (4) is the "double double-time" version of the basic groove.

The terms *half time* and *double time* stand for the following:

The tempo is retained, but the snare accent is on **3** in half time and on all **and** beats in double time.

I have placed the term "*double double time*" in quotation marks, as I am not aware that this term exists as such. I like to use this phrase, however, as it nicely illustrates the effect explained here.

Practice Instructions

Play each groove four times. Although the bass drum and hi-hat are not altered, the groove gains a completely different character through the altered snare position. You should, however, attempt to memorize the sound of the bass drum in the basic groove so that you can also hear it in grooves (2) to (4).

Example 1B uses the same grooves as **Example 1A** but in a different combination of indvidiual grooves. Here, the basic groove is always alternated with one of the other snare positions.

Play each of these grooves four times.

Example 1B

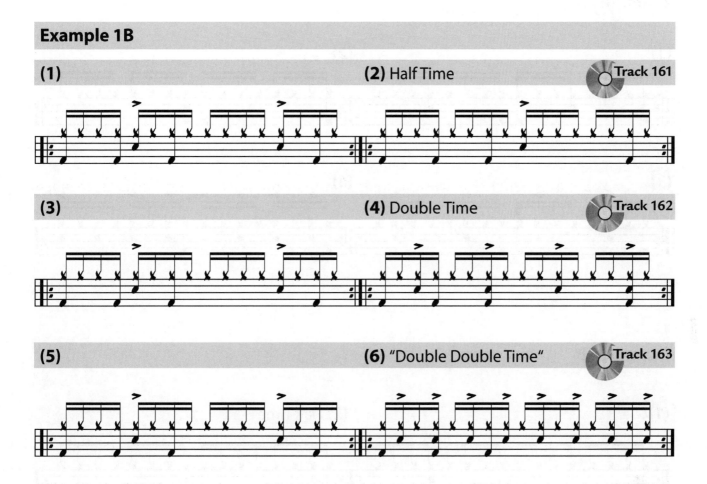

This exercise will give you a good feeling of how much "power" you have over the tempo feeling of your groove with the different placement of the snare, even though the bass drum and hi-hat remain unchanged.

You can employ this concept as a fill when playing with your band. You play, for example, three measures of the basic groove and one measure half time, double time, or even "double double time."

The figure will continue to blend well with the bass, as the bass drum figure remains unchanged and the bass player frequently orients himself to the bass drum.

The grooves notated on the following pages (**Examples 2** to **5**) swiftly increase in level of difficulty, but are all based on the above-explained concept.

Here is another bass drum pattern. **Examples 2A** and **2B** utilize the same bass drum pattern, but are distinguished from one another in the alternation between the basic groove and the variation in **Example 2B**.

Example 2A

(1)   **(2)**

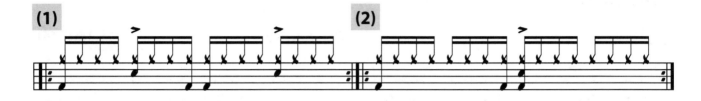

(3)   **(4)**

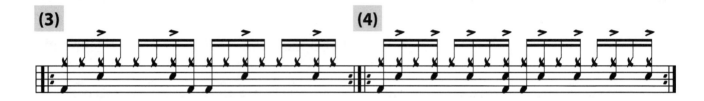

Example 2B

(1)   **(2)** Half Time

(3)   **(4)** Double Time

(5)   **(6)** "Double Double Time"

Here is another bass drum pattern.

Example 3A

(1)   **(2)**

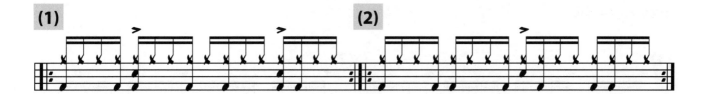

(3)   **(4)**

Example 3B

(1)   **(2)** Half Time

(3)   **(4)** Double Time

(5)   **(6)** "Double Double Time"

Examples 4A und 4B contain an open hi-hat on **4+**. You open the hi-hat on **4+** and close it again on **1**. You will see the sign for opening the hi-hat in the music as an "**o**" on **4+**. The sign for closing the hi-hat is marked in the notation by the "**+**" on the **first beat**.

Example 4A

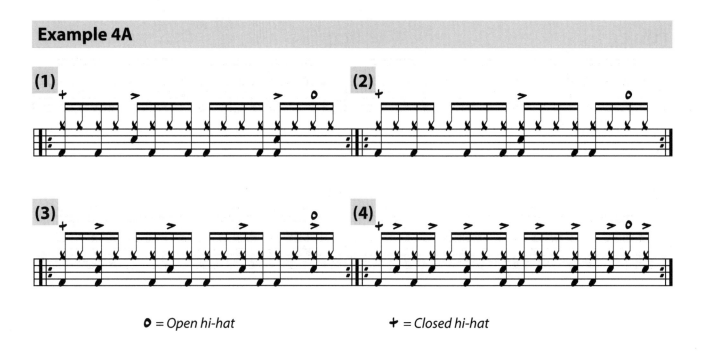

o = Open hi-hat   **+** = Closed hi-hat

Example 4B

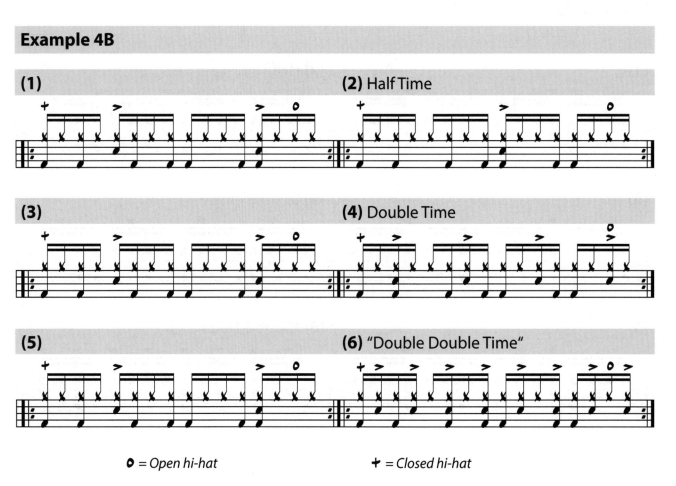

o = Open hi-hat   **+** = Closed hi-hat

In **Examples 5A** and **5B** the hi-hat opening is shorter.

This time, the hi-hat is only open for a sixteenth note. You open the hi-hat on **4a** and close it again on **1**.

The bass drum pattern is also slightly more challenging. When the bass drum is played together with the snare in exercise **(3)** and **(4)**, make sure that you play both instruments exactly at the same time.

Example 5A

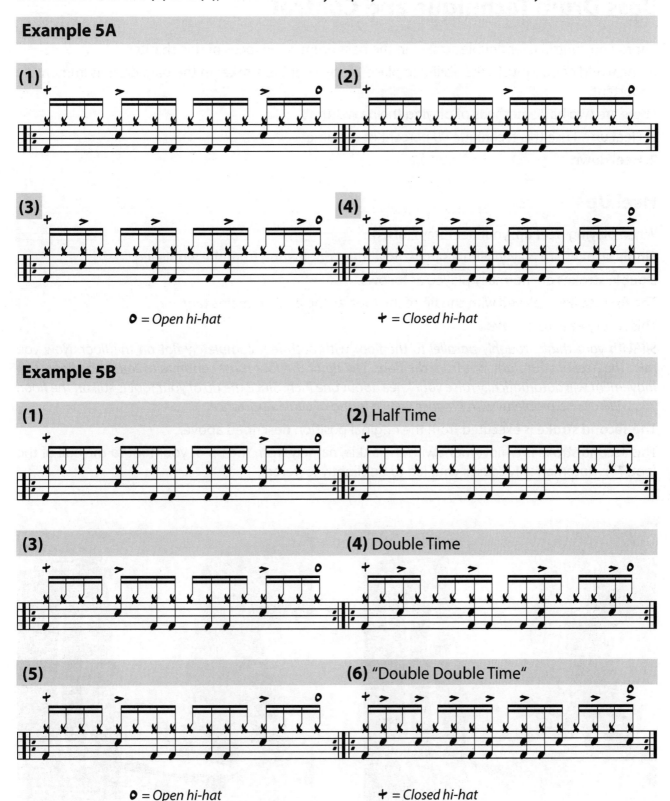

○ = Open hi-hat   **✚** = Closed hi-hat

Example 5B

○ = Open hi-hat   **✚** = Closed hi-hat

If you feel like creating more grooves of this type, you only need to figure out other bass drum patterns, as the hi-hat pattern and placement of the snare remain unchanged.

You will find bass drum patterns in **Reading Text 4 – 16ths (1)** or in **Reading Text 5 – 16ths (2)**.

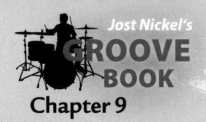

Bass Drum Technique and Control

Improving control over double strokes in the bass drum is the focus of this chapter.

In the world of pop music, the ability to place precise double strokes in the bass drum is immensely important.

There are two basic methods of playing the bass drum.

1. Heel up – I use this technique 99 percent of the time.

2. Heel down

Heel Up

When playing **heel up**, your heel stays raised.

Single strokes are played with a single movement originating from the whole leg.

Double strokes are normally played as follows:

The first stroke is played with the tip of the foot, as the ankle remains taut.

This is very easy to imitate:

Sit with your thighs roughly parallel to the floor with both feet completely flat on the floor. Now you raise the heel of your right foot from the floor. The tip of the foot must continue to touch the floor. This movement will automatically raise your knee about one inch. Since the tip of your foot is still on the floor, you will have no problems with balance, which is also of vital importance.

The second stroke is executed from the original position described above.

This second stroke is a movement with the ankle, namely from the tip of your foot to the ball of the foot. This automatically causes your leg to be slightly lowered.

1st stroke: Tip of the foot

2nd stroke: Ball of the foot

This double-stroke technique will mean that the second of the two beats will always be slightly louder than the first, as the leg moves down on the second beat. This difference in the sound level is explicitly desired!

Tempo

The double-stroke technique described above (two consecutive sixteenth notes) functions best at a minimum speed of about *80 bpm* (*beats per minute*).

In a very slow tempo under about *80 bpm*, I play two consecutive sixteenth notes with two single movements originating from the whole leg. The double-stroke technique described above is too difficult to control in slower tempos.

The tempo indications are only a guideline and correspond to my personal experience.

Exception: There are a few drummers who perform the double-stroke technique described above exactly the other way around, but more than 90 percent utilize the technique as described above.

Seat Height

To adjust the seat height, I sit down at the set and raise both heels off the floor (the tips of the feet are on the pedals). Now I adjust the seat height so that my thighs are parallel to the floor.

However, many drummers are used to sitting much higher or lower, but are still able to play in an excellent way.

"Playing off the Head" Versus Balance

Many drummers leave the **bass drum beater** on the drumhead after a stroke, as this makes it easier to retain their balance. To maintain your balance keep either the tip of your foot on the pedal (with the bass drum beater on the drumhead) or place your heel on the bottom of the pedal so that the beater leaves the drumhead.

The term *playing off the head* means that you move the bass drum beater away from the drumhead immediately after the beat. The reason for this would be to achieve a different sound and tonality from the bass drum. Many drummers attempting to play like this then hold their leg off the ground and, therefore, experience balance problems. This can not only cause discomfort when playing, but also make the exact placement of the strokes very difficult and sometimes even impossible.

The top priority when playing the bass drum with the heel-up technique is that you retain perfect balance throughout. This is the only way to achieve precision.

In my opinion, the sound produced by *playing off the head* is at best only marginally better. Even if the bass drum does sound a little better, your feel for playing and the associated ability to place the beats precisely have much greater priority. Who would ever say the following about a hiring a drummer:

"Drummer 'A' has an amazing bass drum sound, but he plays inaccurately. Drummer 'B' has a great groove, but the bass drum sound is not as good. We are not concerned about groove so we'll go with Drummer 'A'..."

For this reason, do not be over-concerned with playing off the head of the bass drum and concentrate more on accuracy and precision.

If you do, however, really want to play off the head, the best variant is to place your heel down after each beat to prevent losing contact with the floor.

Exception: Playing off the head actually does sound better if you prefer an unmuted, open-sounding bass drum sound, as often used in jazz. For this reason, jazz drummers often play with their heel down.

Heel Down

Here we keep the whole foot on the pedal. The movement originates from the ankle.

The *advantage* of this technique is that you will experience fewer problems with your balance. The *downside* is, however, that you are almost unable to achieve sufficient volume and pressure with your heel down, which is vital in pop music. Fast patterns are also much harder to play the bass drum with your heel down.

Exercises

The following exercises will help you substantially improve your control over double strokes on the bass drum. The idea behind the exercises is that the second note of a double stroke is always the more important one—the **target note**. I feel that the first beat is like an **upbeat** for the second beat.

All exercises in this chapter are built up as follows:

• **The right hand** plays eighth notes on the hi-hat.

• **The left hand** plays the snare on **2** and **4**.

All grooves consist of two measures:

In **measure 1**, the bass drum plays only **single strokes (target notes)** to train your feeling for its position. In **measure 2**, the bass drum plays **double strokes** by adding a sixteenth note on the bass drum immediately **prior** to the target note.

Watch your **dynamics** on double strokes:

The first stroke is softer than the second (*see accents*).

Do not practice the exercises too slowly! The minimum tempo is *80 bpm*!

Exercise 1

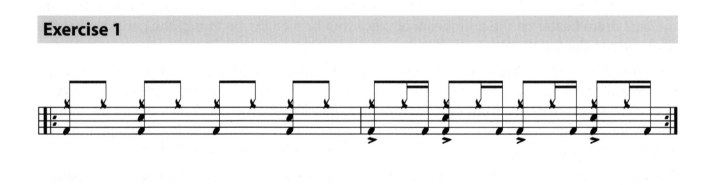

Exercise 2

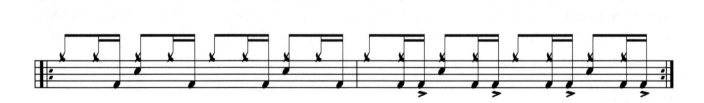

Exercise 3

Exercise 4

> ### Practice Tip
>
> Do not worry if you find **Exercises 1** and **3** easier than **2** and **4**. The majority of drummers will feel the same way. This is because the target notes are on an eighth note.
>
> **To Recall: On the second stroke, your target note, your leg goes down.**
>
> Persevere in practicing the **Exercises 2** and **4** until you find them as easy as **1** and **3**.

Exercise 5 (Eight-Measure Combination of Exercises 1 to 4)

Now we continue with grooves containing double strokes at different positions. Here we will utilize **Reading Text 5 – 16ths (2)** as a source for bass drum strokes.

Although the reading text contains a large number of double strokes, we only play single strokes in the first measure. With the double strokes, only play the target notes (the second stroke of each double stroke). The single strokes are played as notated. In the second measure, we play the complete pattern.

Exercise 6 | Reading Text 5 / Line 3 / Measure 1

target notes

Exercise 7 | Reading Text 5 / Line 4 / Measure 1

Exercise 8 | Reading Text 5 / Line 5 / Measure 1

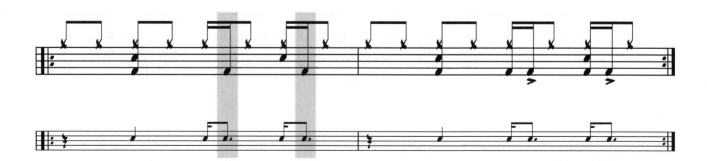

Exercise 9 | Reading Text 5 / Line 6 / Measure 1

If you want to create more bass drum exercises, you can use additional measures from **Reading Text 5** and transform them in the same fashion to improve your bass drum control.

Summary

In double strokes on the bass drum, the second stroke is more important, the so-called **target note**. This note is louder because your leg moves down on the second beat.

In order to figure out the position of these target notes, we practice two-bar grooves in which the **first measure** consists of single strokes and the sixteenth note **prior** to the target note is not added until the second measure.

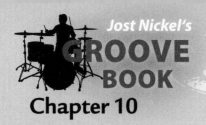

Three-Note Groove Variations

In this chapter, we cover groove variations, which I really like using.

The idea seems unspectacular, but it is highly effective. We take the pattern **RLF** (**Example 3–Note 1A**) and play it on different positions in the groove. I call this variation *3-note* because it consists of three sixteenth notes. We begin with **3-Note 1**:

3-Note 1

| **3-Note 1A** | **3-Note1B** (from 2+ to 3a) | Track 164 |

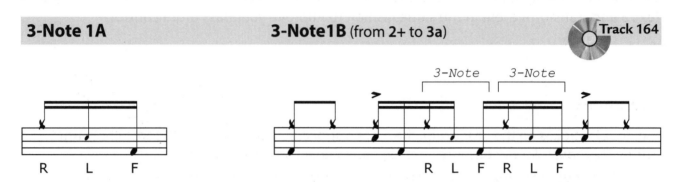

I not only play **Example 1B** as an independent groove, but also use **Example 1B** as a variation on the groove.

3-Note 1C (Three-measure groove with Example 1B in the fourth measure as a variation)

The bass drum pattern is identical in all four measures in **Example 1C**. Try to memorize the sound of the bass drum pattern in the underlying groove so well that you can also hear it in the variation in the fourth measure.

3-Note 1D (from 2e to 4e)   Track 165

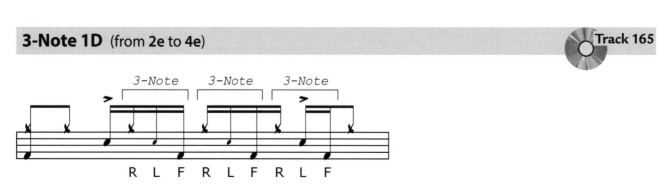

3-Note 1E (Example 1D as variation in measure 4)

R L F R L F R L F

3-Note 1F (from 2 to 3e)   Track 166

R L F R L F R L R

3-Note 1G (Example 1F as variation in measure 4)

R L F R L F R L R

In the following exercise, the different positions of **3-Note 1** are combined with one another. You should first practice each line separately before playing through the whole exercise.

3-Note 1 – Study   Track 167

R L F R L F   R L F R L F

R L F R L F R L F   R L F R L F R L R

R L F R L F   R L F R L F R L F R L F R L R

R L F R L F R   R L F R L F R   R L F R L F R L

3-Note 2

We will alter the pattern by adding a beat with the right hand. As before, the right hand begins on the hi-hat. On the second beat, left and right hands play **simultaneously**.

As before, the third beat comes on the bass drum.

3-Note 2A   **3-Note 2B** (from 2+ to 3a)   Track 168

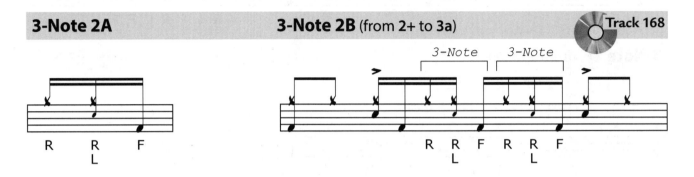

3-Note 2C (Three-measure groove with **Example 2A** in the fourth measure as a variation)

3-Note 2D (from 2e to 4e)   Track 169

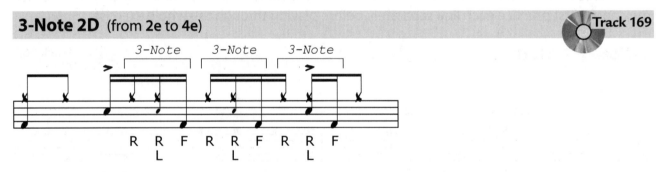

3-Note 2E (Example 2D as a variation in measure 4)

3-Note 2F (from 2a to 3e)   Track 170

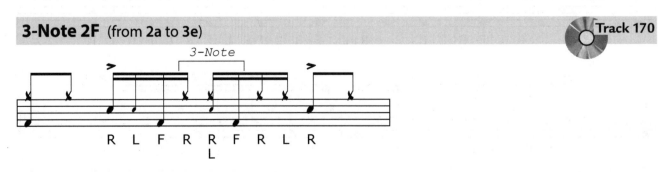

3-Note 2G (Example 2F as a variation in measure 4)

In the following exercise, the different positions of **3-Note 2** are combined with one another. You should first practice each line separately before playing through the whole exercise.

3-Note 2 – Study   Track 171

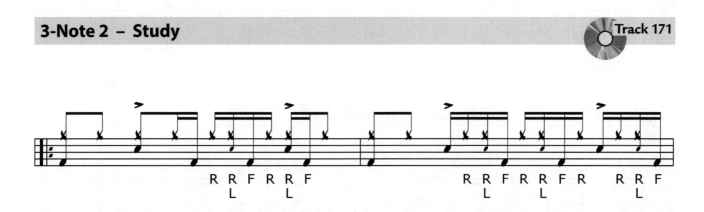

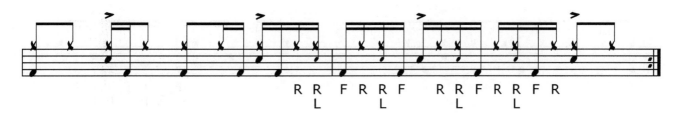

3-Note 3

In **3-Note 3**, it is only the orchestration that is changed: the sticking from **3-Note 2** remains unchanged. The hands are divided as follows:

Beat 1: The right hand plays on the floor tom.
Beat 2: The right hand remains on the floor tom and the left hand plays simultaneously on the hi-hat.
Beat 3: Bass drum

3-Note 3A   **3-Note 3B** (from 2+ to 3a)   Track 172

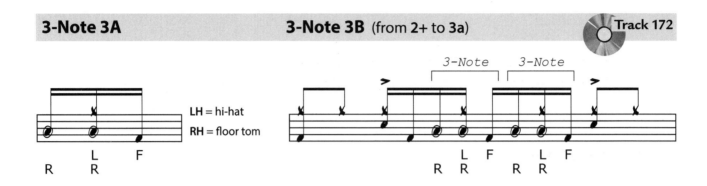

3-Note 3C (Example 3B as a variation in measure 4)

3-Note 3D (from 2e to 4e)   Track 173

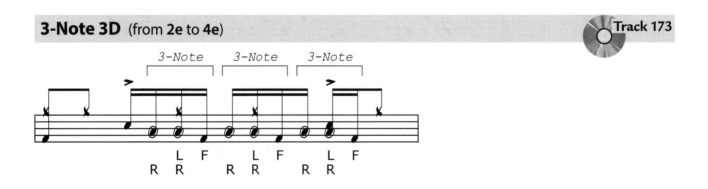

3-Note 3E (Example 3D as a variation in measure 4)

3-Note 3F (from 2a to 3e)

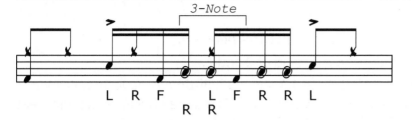

3-Note 3G (Example 3F as a variation in measure 4)

In the following exercise, the different positions of **3-Note 3** are combined with one another. The different hi-hat openings have also been added to make the transitions more elegant.

You should first practice each line separately before playing through the whole exercise.

3-Note 3 – Study

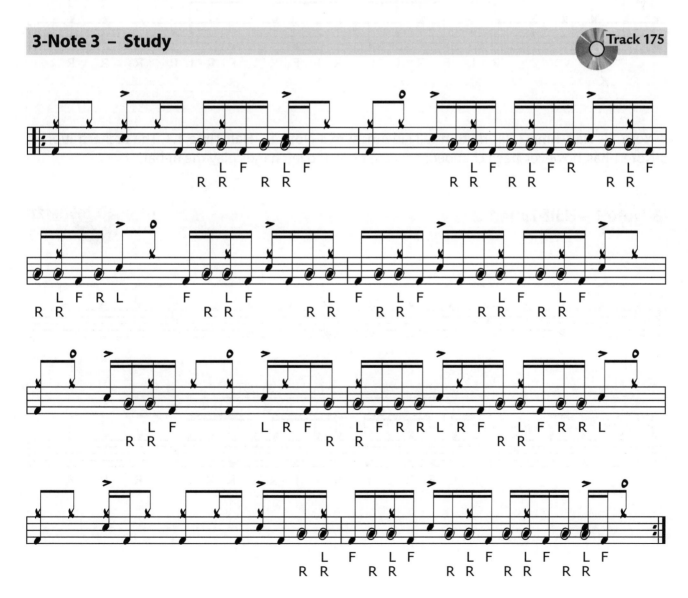

3-Note 1 in Half-Time Grooves

We will now play **3-Note 1** in half-time grooves.

To recall: 3-Note 1 is a group of three notes consisting of **RLF** (*see page 94*).

Half time means that we play the snare accents on **3** instead of **2** and **4**.

Measures 1 and 2 from **Example 3-Note 1 – Half-Time 1.1** show a half-time groove. In measures 3 and 4, we play **3-Note 1** as a variation or a fill. The groove character is retained because the backbeat continues to be played on **3** in measures 3 and 4. **3-Note 1** begins in measure 3 on **3+**.

3-Note 1 – Half-Time 1.1   Track 176

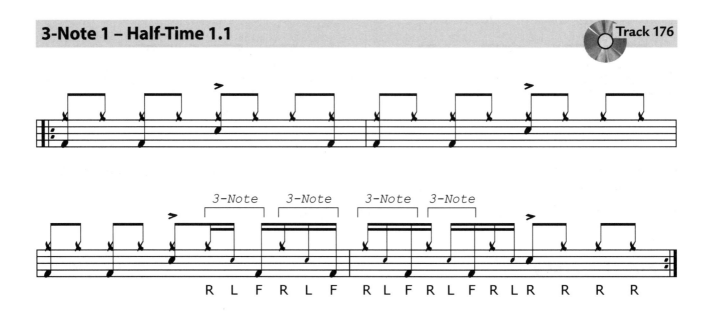

3-Note 1 – Half-Time 1.2 is rhythmically identical to **3-Note 1 – Half-Time 1.1**. The orchestration of 3-Note 1 has, however, been changed: now the right and left hands play the hi-hat.

3-Note 1 – Half-Time 1.2   Track 177

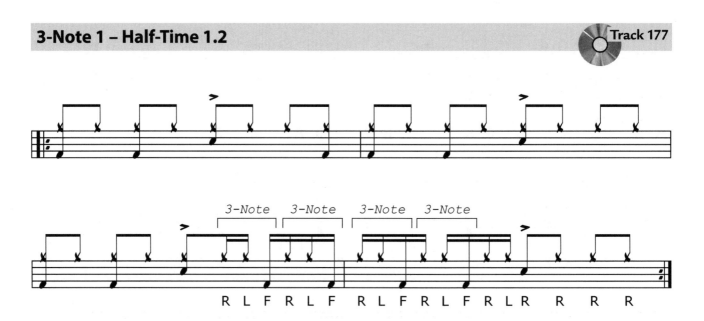

3-Note 1 – Half-Time 1.3 shows a further orchestration of **3-Note 1**.

Here the right and left hands play the toms. The rhythm remains unchanged. You are free to decide which toms you want to play.

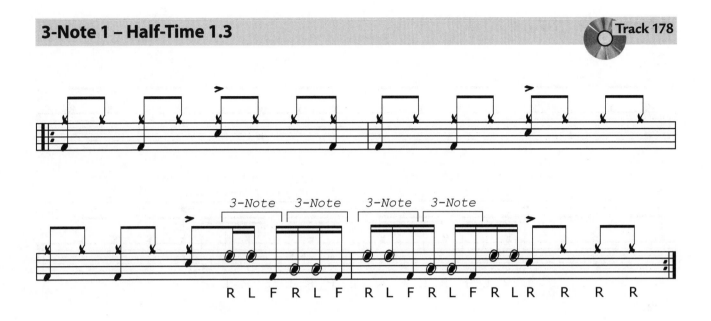

3-Note 1 – Half-Time 1.4 shows a further orchestration of **3-Note 1**.

Here the right hand plays the toms and the left hand plays the hi-hat. The rhythm remains unchanged.

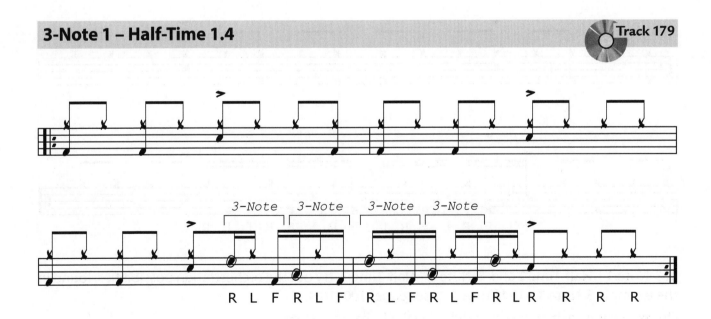

In **3-Note 1 – Half-Time 2**, we alter the position of **3-Note 1** within a half-time context. Measures 1 and 2 have the same half-time groove as before. In measures 3 and 4, we play **3-Note 1**.

3-Note 1, however, already begins on the **3e** in measure 3.

3-Note 1 – Half-Time 2

Track 180

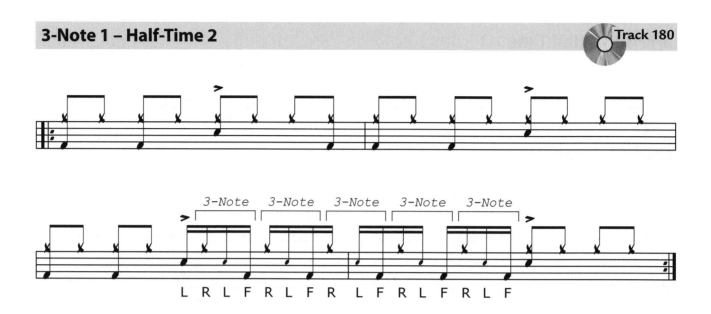

Now we come to the third and final position of **3-Note 1** within a half-time context. Measures 1 and 2 consist of the already familiar half-time groove. In measures 3 and 4, we play **3-Note 1**.

Here, however, the **3-Note 1** already begins on the **3** in measure 3.

3-Note 1 – Half-Time 3

Track 181

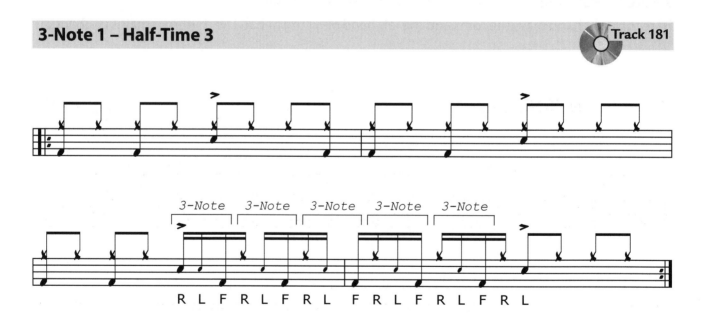

In **3-Note 1 – Half-Time 2** and **3-Note 1 – Half-Time 3**, try out the orchestration possibilities, found in the example **3-Note 1 – Half-Time 1.1** (*see pages 100–101*).

Orchestration variant 1: Both hands play the hi-hat in **3-Note 1**.

Orchestration variant 2: Both hands play toms in **3-Note 1**.

Orchestration variant 3: The right hand plays toms on **3-Note 1** and the left hand plays hi-hat.

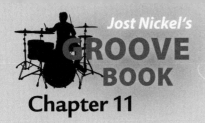
Go-Go Grooves

In this chapter, we take a look at **go-go grooves**. The special feature of this groove is that the right hand plays a pattern over an entire measure.

I usually play the cowbell with the right hand in this groove. If you do not have a cowbell, you can instead use the bell of the ride cymbal. Very rarely, I play these grooves on the hi-hat.

Cowbell Pattern 1

Line 1 shows the cowbell pattern 1 plus snare on **2** and **4**.
Line 2 shows the cowbell positions in a sixteenth-note diagram.

Cowbell Pattern 1

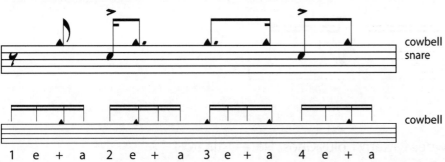

Practice Tip: Before adding the bass drum pattern, practice the cowbell pattern plus snare on **2** and **4** just with your hands.

Now we will add two different bass drum patterns.

Cowbell Pattern 1.1 (Bass Drum Pattern 1)

Track 182

Practice Tip: As the cowbell pattern probably feels strange, add each bass drum beat separately. First play the cowbell pattern plus snare (in an endless loop) and then only the bass drum on **1**. Once you feel comfortable with that, you can add the next bass drum beat on **2a**, etc.

This method of practicing has the advantage that you are playing a groove the whole time, which you are slowly but surely augmenting. Attempting to play the whole groove straightaway can prove frustrating because you repeatedly have to go back to the beginning.

Cowbell Pattern 1.2 (Bass Drum Pattern 2)

Track 183

Cowbell Pattern 1 Plus Ghost Notes

Playing **ghost notes** in go-go grooves is great fun, but somewhat challenging. Here is a good opportunity to integrate ghost notes into these grooves.

In *chapter 5* on ghost notes, I showed you a number of different ghost note ostinatos. We will take **Ghost Note Ostinato 1** (*see page 49*) and add this to the go-go grooves that you already know.

To recall: The left hand plays the following in **Ghost Note Ostinato 1**:

Ghost Note Ostinato 1

Preparatory Exercise (Cowbell Pattern 1 plus Ghost Note Ostinato 1)

Cowbell Pattern 1.3 (Bass Drum Pattern 1 / Ghost Notes)

Cowbell Pattern 1.4 (Bass Drum Pattern 2 / Ghost Notes)

Cowbell Pattern 1 Plus Eighth Note Hi-Hat with the Left Foot

Especially go-go grooves sound good with eighth notes on the hi-hat played by the left foot. The two examples show the two go-go grooves (**Examples 1.3** and **1.4**) with eighths in the hi-hat played with the foot.

Cowbell Pattern 1.5 (Bass Drum Pattern 1 / Ghost Notes / LF–Hi-Hat)  Track 184

Cowbell Pattern 1.6 (Bass Drum Pattern 2 / Ghost Notes / LF–Hi-Hat)  Track 185

Practice Tip: Play **Examples 1.5** and **1.6** consecutively.
• First play four measures of 1.5 followed by four measures of 1.6.
• Then play two measures of 1.5 followed by two measures of 1.6.
• Finally play one measure of 1.5 and one measure of 1.6.

Now you have to consider the next steps. You could naturally spend the rest of your life practicing different bass drum patterns along with **Cowbell Pattern 1**. As the cowbell pattern is the central stylistic element in go-go grooves, I consider it much better to practice other cowbell patterns.

The method in the next cowbell patterns will remain the same. First two different bass drum patterns are added to the cowbell pattern. This is followed by **Ghost Note Ostinato 1** and eighth notes played with the foot on the hi-hat.

Cowbell Pattern 2

Now we continue with **Cowbell Pattern 2**. This pattern is a decorated form of **Cowbell Pattern 1** with three beats added. These beats are marked with an asterisk (*) and occur on beats 2, 3e, and 4a.

Cowbell Pattern 2

Line **1** shows **Cowbell Pattern 2** plus snare on **2** and **4**.
Line **2** shows the cowbell positions in a sixteenth-note diagram.

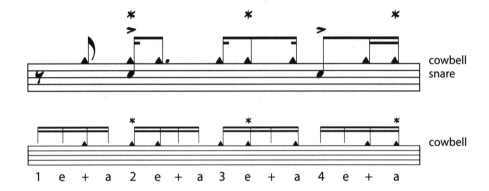

Next we add the **Bass Drum Patterns 1** and **2** as in **Cowbell Pattern 1**.

Practice Tip: Remember the practice tips on *page 103*!

Cowbell Pattern 2.1 (Bass Drum Pattern 1)

Track 186

Cowbell Pattern 2.2 (Bass Drum Pattern 2)

Track 187

Cowbell Pattern 2 Plus Ghost Notes

We also play this pattern with **Ghost Note Ostinato 1** and **Bass Drum Patterns 1** and **2**.

Preparatory Exercise (Cowbell Pattern 2 plus Ghost Note Ostinato 1)

Cowbell Pattern 2.3 (Bass Drum Pattern 1 / Ghost Notes)

Cowbell Pattern 2.4 (Bass Drum Pattern 2 / Ghost Notes)

Cowbell Pattern 2 Plus Eighth Note Hi-Hat with the Left Foot

Cowbell Pattern 2.5 (Bass Drum Pattern 1 / Ghost Notes / LF–Hi-Hat)    Track 188

Cowbell Pattern 2.6 (Bass Drum Pattern 2 / Ghost Notes / LF–Hi-Hat)    Track 189

Cowbell Pattern 3

Now we progress to **Cowbell Pattern 3**, which is derived from **Cowbell Pattern 1** (*see page 103*).

We displace **Cowbell Pattern 1** by a half measure and this then becomes **Cowbell Pattern 3**. The **third beat** of Cowbell Pattern 1 becomes the **first beat** of Cowbell Pattern 3.

Cowbell Pattern 3

Line 1 shows **Cowbell Pattern 1** over two measures.
Line 2 shows **Cowbell Pattern 3**.
Line 3 shows the cowbell positions in a sixteenth-note diagram.

Cowbell Pattern 1

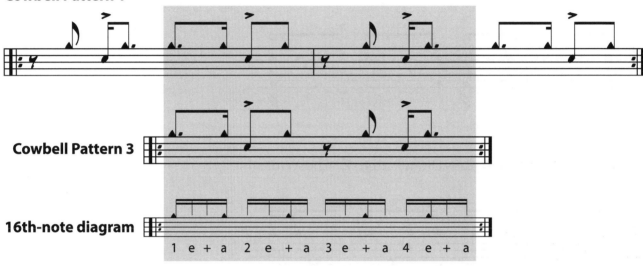

In these cowbell patterns, we also limit ourselves to two different bass drum patterns, which I have selected for you, as they both sound really good.

Cowbell Pattern 3.1 (Bass Drum Pattern 3)

Cowbell Pattern 3.2 (Bass Drum Pattern 4)

Cowbell Pattern 3 Plus Ghost Notes and Eighth Note Hi-Hat with the Left Foot

The next two examples show **Cowbell Pattern 3** plus **Ghost Note Ostinato 1** *and* **pedaled hi-hat.**

Practice Tip: If you find it difficult to add ghost notes and the pedaled hi-hat in a single stage, begin by only adding the ghost notes to **Cowbell Pattern 3**, then adding the bass drum, and finally adding the pedaled hi-hat.

Cowbell Pattern 3.3 (Bass Drum Pattern 3 / Ghost Notes / LF–Hi-Hat)

Cowbell Pattern 3.4 (Bass Drum Pattern 4 / Ghost Notes / LF–Hi-Hat)

Cowbell Pattern 4

Now we come to the fourth and final cowbell pattern. This is the ornamented form of **Cowbell Pattern 3** to which three beats are added. These beats are marked with an asterisk (*) and occur on beats **1e**, **2a**, and **4**.

Cowbell Pattern 4

Line 1 Cowbell Pattern 4 plus snare on **2** and **4**.
Line 2 shows the cowbell positions in a sixteenth-note diagram.

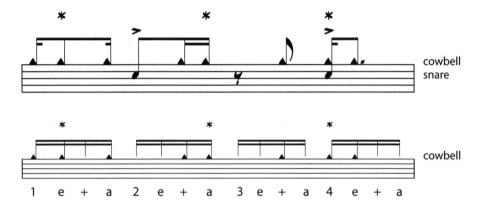

Now we play **Bass Drum Patterns 3** and **4** with **Cowbell Pattern 4**.

Cowbell Pattern 4.1 (Bass Drum Pattern 3)

Cowbell Pattern 4.2 (Bass Drum Pattern 4)

We also round off these grooves with **Ghost Note Ostinato 1** and the pedaled hi-hat.

Practice Tip: If you find it difficult to add ghost notes and the pedaled hi-hat in a single stage, begin by only adding the ghost notes to **Cowbell Pattern 4**, then adding the bass drum, and finally adding the pedaled hi-hat.

Cowbell Pattern 4.3 (Bass Drum Pattern 3 / Ghost Notes / LF–Hi-Hat)

Cowbell Pattern 4.4 (Bass Drum Pattern 4 / Ghost Notes / LF–Hi-Hat)

At the end of this chapter, we finally come to our freestyle exercise!

The following go-go groove studies are all based on **Cowbell Patterns 1** to **4**.

In these grooves, you will encounter a few new bass drum patterns. Additionally, we have intertwined ghost notes (*see Chapter 5, pages 52–53*) and a few displaced snare accents (*see Chapter 7, pages 71–81*).

Practice Tip: All grooves are notated with eighth notes pedaled on the hi-hat. If you find it difficult to play the complete groove straightaway, here are a number of possibilities for approaching this groove:

1. Only play cowbell and snare (just with your hands).

2. Play cowbell and snare plus the bass drum. Begin by playing a few measures only with the first bass drum beat, then a few measures with the first two bass drum beats, and continue until the bass drum pattern is complete.

3. Play in a four-bar alternation first, only with your hands, and then with your hands plus the complete bass drum pattern.

4. Only play the bass drum and the pedaled hi-hat (just with your feet).

5. In a final step, play the complete groove in a four-bar alternation with and without the pedaled hi-hat.

Cowbell Pattern 1 – Study

(1)

(2)

(3)

Cowbell Pattern 2 – Study

(1)

(2)

(3)

Cowbell Pattern 3 – Study

(1)   Track 200

(2)   Track 201

(3)   Track 202

Cowbell Pattern 4 – Study

(1)   Track 203

(2)   Track 204

(3)   Track 205

(4)   Track 206

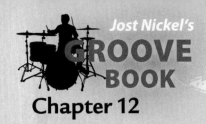

Chapter 12

Timing, Groove, and Philosophy

The twelfth and final chapter is devoted to the topics **timing, groove, and philosophy.**

I could, of course, have placed my thoughts on this thematic concept at the beginning of this book, but recalling how I used to work with textbooks, I decided against it. More often than not, I didn't bother to read the texts, but just got straight into reading and playing the music.

Because of the players who want to get playing straightaway, I have placed this chapter at the end of the volume. I do, however, hope you go about things differently than I used to and actually read through this text!

It is far easier to express the meaning of the word *timing* than the meaning of *groove*.

If you describe a musician as having *good timing*, this means that he is able to sustain a tempo well, neither speeding up nor slowing down (e.g. a song begins at *98 bpm* and runs through in this exact tempo until the end). You can measure this with a *metronome* or, alternatively, play along to a metronome beat.

In contrast, the word *groove* describes an emotion. If something *grooves well*, it simply feels good. A good groove moves most individuals on a direct emotional level.

If you are on a search for a *good groove*, you have to look for a *good feeling*. If you are on the search for *good timing*, you need a *drum computer*. A good groove originates within yourself! If you feel good playing a particular tempo or pattern, this feeling will communicate itself not only to your fellow musicians, but, ultimately, to your public.

You will find exercises to help you work on developing a better feeling for grooves in the practice section of this chapter, beginning on *page 119*.

The topic groove is therefore a highly individual subject area. You have to rely on your feelings when evaluating grooves, and this explains why many individuals are unsure and ask themselves: *"Is this proper grooving? Or perhaps not?"*

The positive feeling often generated by making music is probably one of the main reasons humans enjoy making music so much—this certainly applies to myself!

Philosophy

In my opinion, there is a fundamental difference between *practicing* and *playing concerts or recording*.

When I am practicing, I devote myself to things I cannot yet do or things I don't feel as great about as I should. I take a highly analytic approach to this topic (*see the practice section in this chapter beginning on page 119*).

When I am performing, my chief focus is on feeling good at that particular moment. I play things that I can do in my sleep (because I have practiced them well) or something that develops out of an improvisation almost without thinking.

Ideally, I don't think!

However, this doesn't always go according to plan!

Unproductive thoughts could include the following:

"Didn't this groove better yesterday?"; "Is the tempo right?"; "Are we faster (or slower) now?"; "What fill am I going to play next?"; "Why are my fellow musicians or that guy in the crowd looking at me like that?"; "Is that perhaps boring?"; "Did he just play a dud note?" or *"Oh, no! I've just played a dud note!"* etc.

If I notice that a devil is perching on my shoulder and whispering destructive thoughts to me, I respond directly with unfriendly words.

Alternatively, I focus my attention on other things. I listen, for example, especially to the sound of my hi-hat or concentrate on what one of the other members of the band is playing at this particular moment.

The ideal concept of playing without thinking is unfortunately not easy to achieve—first because of your own sometimes destructive thoughts (*see above*), and second because drummers are frequently the target in matters of scattered tempo or "bad" timing.

The drummer naturally has a particularly large responsibility for tempo, timing, and dynamics: he does not have the sole responsibility, but shares it with all members of the band. Rhythm is the level on which all musicians communicate with each other. Every single musical contribution within a song has a rhythmic relationship. Everyone involved is collectively responsible for the groove and timing, but we drummers bear the greatest portion of responsibility.

In the early days, if someone had asked me in rehearsal when playing through a piece:

"Did that just get faster?" I used to think: *"The world is coming to an end … I got faster …!"*

Nowadays, I merely say: *"Maybe it did, but it wasn't deliberate."*

Perfect Timing?

A good musical performance is not necessarily one in which the timing is perfect. And: *Perfect timing does not automatically make a good performance.*

In my opinion, you can safely get faster or slower as long as everything feels good. There are two very successful and super groovy songs that speed up considerably during performance:

1. "September" by **Earth, Wind & Fire** and
2. "Street Life" by **The Crusaders**.

You really ought to listen to the studio recordings of these songs. When you have listened to one of them, go back to the beginning—you will realize how much the tempo has increased in both of these songs. But are they "bad" performances because of that? Certainly not! Is the groove missing because of this? Definitely not!

You can be sure that the musicians noticed that they were all speeding up together. They may even have produced several additional versions in which they didn't speed up. In the end, however, they chose the version that sounds and grooves the best, even if the tempo was not 100 percent constant.

This is not to say that good timing is not important. It does, however, mean that good music cannot be purely defined by its technical parameters.

I believe that some musicians become obsessed with perfect timing because it is so easy to check. This means they are impeded by rational criteria instead of devotion to the much vaguer field of emotion and expression in music. The reason could be simple: you have to be confident of your own taste in order to focus on it.

Playing Live with a Click?

When playing live, I basically play without clicks.

I do have a metronome that helps me count in in the right tempo. Straight after one song, I listen to the tempo of the next song, concentrate on the part of the song that most influences the tempo to be selected, and then count in the band. Here, I mostly use the hi-hat, because on larger stages the other musicians cannot hear the counts with sticks as well. My fellow musicians are normally able to hear the hi-hat via their monitor boxes or in-ear monitoring in their headphones.

It can, however, still happen that some members of the band have a different idea of the tempo than I do and perhaps want to play faster than my introductory counts. As I play without click, it is easier for me to react to this. The band then sounds more homogenous because I am better able to interact with them rather than having to retain the click tempo.

This process is perhaps slightly less exact than computer-generated perfect timing, but without the click I have more musical possibilities, whereas the tempo always remains constant with the click. I would rather go for more musical possibilities!

Admittedly, numerous bands play live with click. Here I am not telling you, *"Do not do this,"* but encouraging you to trust your own timing.

Keep working on it! It will improve constantly over time! You will also progressively get to know yourself better.

One of the most wonderful aspects of making music is that the journey never comes to an end.

There are naturally situations in which I play with a click. Most studio recordings are made with a click. If drum loops are played during a concert, I naturally also have to play with a click as the computer does not listen to me. This means that if the band decides to play a little faster, the computer says: *"No way!"*

There are also situations in which the band leader insists on playing with a click. That is also OK.

Tempo and Adrenaline

The great thing about concerts is that all musicians have more adrenaline in their blood than otherwise. This, however, also means that tempos are basically perceived differently. This is particularly noticeable when playing with a click. Suddenly the tempo that was always great in the rehearsal room sounds much slower.

If you play the concert without a click, everything probably seems fine, but you often unconsciously play the pieces faster than in the rehearsal room.

The "Right" Live Tempo

There are *two* different methods of determining the "right" tempo:

1. For some musicians, the right tempo is what feels good when playing.

For these musicians, it is not that important how their concert sounds on a recording. Even if the tempos are all faster (which is mostly the case), their direct emotions during the concert are far more important than the "correct" tempo.

2. The other approach is that the tempo on the recording is more important than the live moment.

In this case, you attempt to harmonize your emotions during performance with the emotions when listening to the recording. In certain circumstances, you can feel that everything felt good and just right, but when listening to the recording you think: *"That is actually too fast or too slow."* When the next concert comes around, you attempt to play the relevant pieces slightly faster or slower, as appropriate.

That can naturally mean that you play the next concert less "spontaneously" and think more about it. In my opinion, this thinking process is unavoidable for a while to improve your own live tempo. I have listened to very many of my concerts in order to harmonize my feelings while playing and my feelings while listening. I would also recommend that you do the same. Record your concerts and, if possible, try and listen to them on the next day, while the memory of the concert is fresh in your mind. Be critical but not too hard on yourself!

Playing Laid-Back, On Top, or On the Beat?

The three terms *laid-back*, *on top*, and *on the beat* can generate much confusion.

In principle, *laid-back* refers to playing *behind the beat*, *on top* is playing *before the beat*, and *on the beat* means—as it sounds—playing *exactly on the beat*.

These terms only make sense if they are applied to the interaction of several musicians together. A single musician cannot be ahead of something that is not actually there.

Let us imagine that I am going to play a very simple groove with a bassist. I play a groove in eighth notes as below and my colleague on the bass only plays on the **first beat**:

If the bassist plays, for example, more on top (i.e. earlier) than I do, I would ask him to play his note more laid-back (i.e. later).

In the studio, you often encounter discussions about playing laid-back, on top, and on the beat. The studio provides the opportunity to listen to recordings and realize with your own ears what these terms mean. Musicians with good timing are able to adapt quickly to the groove feelings of others without their performances losing bite.

Within this context, I find *three points* particularly important:

1. I have deliberately written "with your own ears" and not "with your own eyes" above. Now that they can actually see where the beats are in the studio, some people have stopped using their own ears. I don't care what my groove looks like! I am far more interested in how it sounds!

2. If you are recording with a click, listen to the recording without the click to judge it. Ultimately, you will not hear the click on the CD. This is why it is primarily important how the band sounds and not whether the drums are on the click. In most sessions I only regard the click as a mode of orientation. Especially when I am recording with other musicians and am the only person who can

hear the click, the others frequently want to play the chorus a little faster. In this situation, I lean more towards a homogenous recording and, as a result, play before the click.

3. If I am playing along with programmed parts (for example, drum loops), I play exactly to them and have no freedom to move away from the click.

If you are playing a piece in a studio, feel the tempo is too slow, and, consequently, are playing too far ahead, I have the following tip for you:

Tip: *Request a tempo in your headphones that is a few (between three and five) beats slower than the actual song tempo, and take a few minutes to play the different parts of the song in the slower tempo. Once you feel good about the slower tempo, return to the old tempo and the recording, and you will find that you will no longer play ahead of tempo. After having spent a few minutes adjusting to the slower tempo, you will now feel that the original tempo that you previously thought was too slow is now really good.*

This process also works excellently if the entire band is playing too far ahead. This trick naturally also functions in the opposite direction:

If you feel that a piece is too fast, play it even faster for a few minutes and then return to the previous tempo; you will not find it too fast now.

Generally, the tendency to play ahead of tempo is very common. You are probably always aiming for a punchy performance but must first learn not to create this energy through a faster tempo. If you therefore come to the chorus of a song that should really "take off," it is frequently sufficient just to open the hi-hat or play the snare louder without actually increasing the tempo.

Basically, I consider the hype surrounding playing *laid-back*, *on top*, or *on the beat* to be exaggerated. Ultimately, every musician will groove according to his individual personality and groove concept. What is important is to remain sensitive, always listen carefully, and sharpen the senses. I sometimes suspect that some musicians and producers only utilize these terms to unnerve others, just as some people always use foreign terms just to show off how well-educated they are.

On a more positive note, these terms represent the legitimate attempt to describe how a musician grooves. If someone says, *"The drummer XY always plays laid-back well,"* this means that this musician has a relaxed way of playing grooves.

These terms can additionally help to organize playing together.

The bands in which musicians listen well to each other and possess a similar groove feeling are the ones that sound best. This shared understanding for timing and grooves will develop best through playing lots of rehearsals and concerts together and less by endless discussion of the topic.

Tempo Anecdotes

As already mentioned, I fundamentally play live *without a click*. When playing with **Jan Delay** (popular German hip-hop artist), I did, however, play one certain song with a click because I repeatetly received comments from bandmembers on the tempo of that song. Some found it too fast and others too slow.

In response, I then spontaneously played the song "Oh Jonny" *with a click* without telling anyone in the band. At one concert, some band members appeared to have an extra-high level of adrenaline in their blood. That evening, I counted in, the band started playing, and the tempo was exactly the same as it had been for the last few gigs, but Jan interrupted the song after the intro, saying: *"That is really too slow!"* I naturally laughed—this was simply not true from a mathematical point of view, but we were making music and not math! We played the piece slightly faster that evening.

After the concert, another member of the band came to me saying, *"But that was really slower than usual."* I couldn't help revealing that I had been the only one playing the song along with a click: The response was: *"Oh! Then it must have been our fault."*

This story is a further indication that the sense of tempo is dependent on a number of different factors and that tempos can be evaluated differently according to individual situations.

On a different tour, I had the following experience. We were all playing with InEar, and the musical director asked me to count in using my drum computer instead of sticks or the hi-hat. The band could hear my drum computer in their earphones and began playing together after the two-measure count-in (which was naturally inaudible to the audience). To ensure that we actually played the songs in the same tempo as the count-in, the idea was that the drum computer would continue for eight measures after the count-in, but that we would play without click from then onwards. All members of the band had excellent timing, but this still didn't work out well, as I was the only one listening to the click during the song. The musicians all had a different sense of tempo, which made it feel strange to me to play the first eight measures (with click), as part of the band deviated from the tempo as counted in. It would have been much better if we had heard the click much louder, but nobody wanted that ... After a few concerts, I altered the count-in so that the drum computer stopped after the count-in. I found it more important that we played together rather than whether we had selected the "correct" tempo.

If playing a concert with a click is necessary, doing so functions best if all musicians can hear the click and are extremely disciplined. The question is, however, how much discipline will the emotions that are transported on stage take. It is ultimately emotion that will impress the audience.

The rehearsal room is a very good place for hard work and discipline (broad hint!)—we will now continue with concrete exercises.

Timing and Groove Exercise 1

In principle, any form of practicing grooves will improve your timing and the quality of your grooves. If you want to concentrate especially on the topic of timing, you should play patterns that are technically easy, permitting you to concentrate fully on your timing and grooves.

We will take simple eighth-note grooves (**Groove Examples 1** to **3**, *see pages 120 and 121*) and play them in a variety of tempos between *60 bpm* and *180 bpm*. Alongside the apparent easiness of eighth-note grooves, the good thing about them is that you can play them within such a wide tempo spectrum (*60 to 180*) without having to alter the pattern.

It probably goes without saying that you should definitely practice these exercises with a click. I find a drum computer to be the best alternative. This is far more suitable than a normal metronome or laptop for a number of reasons.

To improve your timing, just playing along with a quarter-note click is not sufficient. The drum computer will undertake responsibility for the tempo, but you should be doing that yourself.

What we need are **click patterns** with extended breaks, during which the drum computer continues to run but remains silent. You continue playing during these breaks and, with a bit of practice, will maintain the correct tempo when the drum computer resumes its clicks.

I practice timing with a number of different click patterns ...

Click Pattern 1

The click is set to quarter notes.

Click Pattern 2

The click runs in quarter notes in measure 1, and the drum computer is silent during the second measure.

Click Pattern 3

The click only occurs on **beat 1** of the first measure and is otherwise silent.

Once you have programmed these three click patterns in your drum computer, you are ready to go. I always use a cowbell for the sound, as its penetrating tone is always easy to hear.

Here is the first groove in eighth notes for **Timing and Groove Exercise 1**:

Groove 1

Practice Instructions

Select **click pattern 1** in your drum computer and set the tempo to *60 bpm*. Now play the groove again and again until you feel secure with the click. Then you switch to **click pattern 2**. Here the drum computer will only play clicks in the first measure: in the second measure, you alone are responsible for the tempo. As a final stage, switch to **click pattern 3** (while continuing to play). This click pattern will not provide you with any help in keeping the correct tempo: you have exclusive responsibility.

If you notice that you are not yet able to sustain the tempo, keep switching between the different click patterns.

Utilize the tempos that I have compiled in the list below. If you practice according to this plan, you will soon notice which tempos you find easy and which are trickier. You must, of course, practice the tempos that you do not yet find comfortable.

Do not drive yourself crazy with these exercises! Practicing twenty minutes a day as described is quite sufficient, but make sure you give each tempo the time it needs.

If you only practice three different tempos in twenty minutes on a single day, that is no problem. You are not meant to play all tempos in the list in one day, but instead, each tempo until you feel comfortable with it. For example, if you only reach a tempo of *70* on one day, you can continue at *73* the next day.

Tempo List (*bpm*)				
60	62	64	66	68
70	73	76	79	
82	85	88		
91	94	97		
100	104	108		
112	116			
120	125			
130	135			
140	145			
150	155			
160	165			
170	175			
180				

Groove Examples 2 and **3** contain two additional grooves that are excellently suited to the described exercise.

Groove 2

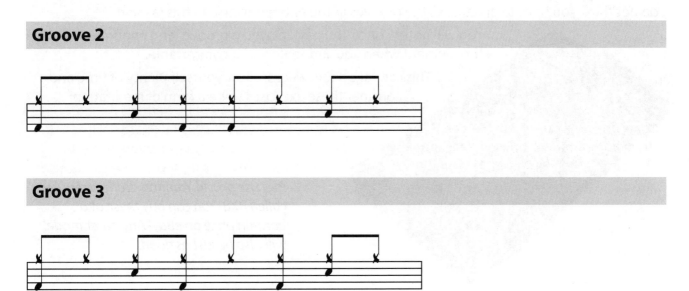

Groove 3

Timing and Groove Exercise 2

Most drummers understand *practice* as a confrontation with *technical difficulties*: this can, for example, be exercises to train independence, new fills, or new grooves.

You should also practice grooves that contain few or even no technical difficulties, but that do not yet feel really good when played.

To make a groove really groove, you must feel yourself absolutely as one with it.

You will learn most from the grooves with which you feel least familiar. If you stumble on one of these grooves while playing in your band, you should take this groove and practice it at the speed at which you also play it with them. It is important to practice precisely the same tempo, as you might be able to play this pattern really well in other tempos, but not in this specific tempo.

Practice Is Repetition!

For this reason, you should take the relevant groove in the especially difficult tempo and play it for around twenty minutes without a break. At the beginning you can practice along with **Click Patterns 1–3**. Once you are able to hold the tempo, you can stop the drum computer, but then switch it on again after a few minutes whilst still playing. When you restart the drum computer, you should set it to **Click Pattern 1** to hear immediately if you have adhered to the tempo.

If you notice, for example, that you have become slower, try the groove somewhat faster the next time. This adjustment of your timing is extremely instructive!

Timing and Groove Exercise 3

A good groove exercise is to play along with CDs. Once you have played for a while with the CD, try playing the same groove without the CD to test whether the good groove feeling remains when the CD is not playing and is therefore not providing any help. If you notice that you are having difficulties with this, you should then practice the same groove in the tempo of the CD along with **Click Patterns 1–3** and then progress as described in **Timing and Groove Exercise 2**:

You switch off the click for a certain period of time, continue playing, and then switch the click back on with **Click Pattern 1**.

Practice Tip: If you spend around *20 minutes* every day on your **Timing and Groove Exercises**, you will substantially improve your groove and timing.

The more grooves you practice in this way, the more you will also improve all other grooves, so do not think you have to practice all the grooves in the entire universe in this fashion.

You will notice, once you have played a groove long enough, the moment when you suddenly find it comfortable.

This can take a few weeks: allow yourself plenty of time and consider these exercises to be a form of meditation!

PS: I use an old Yamaha drum computer called RX8. You can buy these at a bargain price on eBay! Any other model will also be just as good.

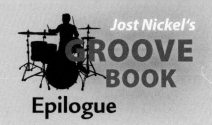
As we near the end of this book, I would like to cover *three more points*.

1. In many grooves in this book, the right hand plays eighth notes on the hi-hat, particularly in *Chapters 5, 6, 7,* and *10*. It is also worthwhile playing other hi-hat or ride patterns along with all these grooves. Here are my **Top 6**:

Hi-Hat and Ride Patterns

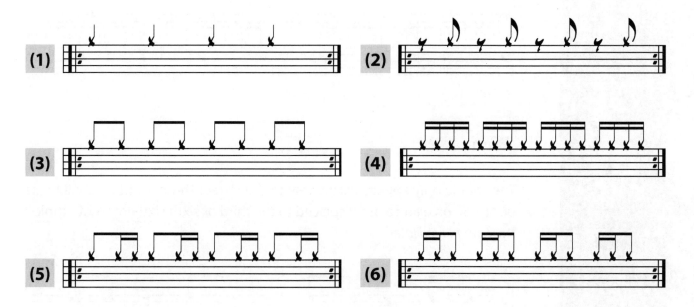

You can also play **Patterns 3–6** with:

- Accents on downbeats
- Accents on offbeats
- Accents on all eighth notes

2. You can also interpret all grooves in this volume as triplets, i.e. shuffled. This particularly applies to *Chapters 1, 2, 3, 4, 10,* and *11*.

3. If you want to play a straight or binary groove shuffled, i.e. in triplets, you must first alter the *division* or *subdivision* of your groove from sixteenth notes to *sixteenth-note triplets*. The quarter notes in shuffled grooves are divided into six (sixteenth-note triplets) and not into four (sixteenth notes).

This **QR code** will lead you to a *video*, in which I play one of the go-go grooves shuffled (*see page 107 / Cowbell Pattern 2.6*).

Although this is a triplet interpretation of grooves, meaning that the notation is not altered, the three examples below will help to clarify the interpretation.

Example 1

All beats that fall on eighth-note downbeats remain *unchanged*.

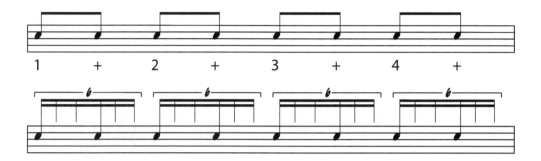

Example 2

The shuffle only applies exclusively to the sixteenth-note offbeats! All beats occurring on **e** and **a** are displaced to the third or sixth sixteenth-note triplet; they are *played later*.

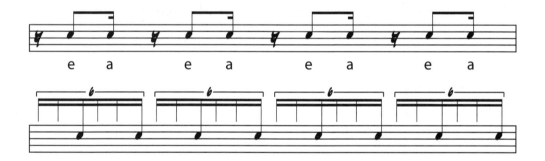

Example 3

With the aid of these patterns, you can see that all downbeats remain unchanged, whereas the offbeats are displaced and *occur later*.

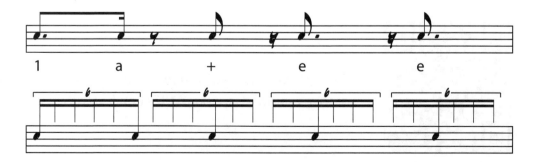

Write down your own grooves on the following four pages.

1. Grooves with interrupted/intertwined sixteenth-note patterns (*see page 33*).

2. Linear Grooves (*see page 42*).

3. Ghost Note Grooves (*see page 56*).

Reading Text 1 – Bass Drum and Snare (1)

1.

2.

3.

4.

5.

6.

7.

8.

9.

10.

Reading Text 2 – Bass Drum and Snare (2)

1.

2.

3.

4.

5.

6.

7.

8.

9.

10.

Reading Text 1 – Bass Drum and Snare (1)

1.

2.

3.

4.

5.

6.

7.

8.

9.

10.

Reading Text 2 – Bass Drum and Snare (2)

1.

2.

3.

4.

5.

6.

7.

8.

9.

10.